THE POWER WITHIN

HOW CAN I CONCENTRATE
WHEN THERE'S FOOD IN FRONT OF ME —
A JOURNEY OF CHANGE

TRENT HEPPLER

How I transformed from being morbidly obese
to running a marathon within a year.
I lost 140 lbs with **NO** surgery,
NO special diet, and **NO** gym membership.

TABLE OF CONTENTS

INTRODUCTION

THE EVE OF my 40th birthday I was morbidly obese. 10 months later I ran my first marathon. I lost more than 140 lbs. without surgery, a special diet, or a gym membership. What the crap did I do? How did I do it? What was I thinking?

Intent:

I WANT TO share my journey from this year in my life. Much of the information shared is pulled straight from my journal as I documented my journey. Many people have asked me "How did you do it?" or "What are you doing?" I've even gotten some people that I've known for years say, "Hi, I'm Steve, nice to meet you" – as if they didn't know who I was.

When people ask me how I accomplished this my response is, "Diet and exercise and changing everything about my life." These encounters have made me feel like my journey of change needs to be shared on a broader spectrum. My hope is to help others in their search for health and wellness in body, mind, and spirit.

I need to share this story to keep myself accountable and make sure I continue to fight the battle that plays out in my head everyday. I share this **personal** transformation so that others may receive direction, encouragement, and inspiration in their own journey of change. In addition to that, I want to preserve a record for my family. Please note that there are many journal entries present in this work. Some have been summarized, but none were edited, in hopes of maintaining the raw and very real feeling they possess.

Background:

I WOULD LIKE to share the first 40 years of my life. I have been a member of The Church of Jesus Christ of Latter-Day Saints my entire life. I will naturally reference situations and share things in "Mormon lingo." If there is something that is hard to understand and is not clarified, I apologize.

♪ "Let's start at the very beginning" ♪ I am the youngest of 7 kids. I have 5 older sisters and 1 older brother. Looking back I realize being the youngest child contributed to how I developed as a human, it is important that you understand that it is part of the reason I am the way I am. My family is close and we get along for the most part. On occasion, there are issues, but that is because we are real people. When it comes right down to it, we love each other.

I have amazing parents; they have provided for me mentally, physically, and spiritually. They are best parents in the world. I know many say that, but mine really are!

All of my siblings were athletic growing up. They all competed in high school sports, or cheer, or dance. Two of them were good enough to compete in college. A few of my siblings even guided river-rafting trips down the Colorado River during their college summer breaks.

At eight years old, I started to grow vertically, and horizontally, unlike any of my other siblings. I started getting rolls and "little boobies", which made playing hard to do because I was chunky. My mom's nickname for me was Honcho, which I liked, but always had a "heavy" connotation to me. I played the role of the fat kid very well. For the rest of grade school, middle school, and high school I was the "fat friend" and almost always the fattest one in class – you know what I mean. I remember breaking the 200 lb. mark in 7th or 8th grade. You were either that person, or you knew who that person was. I learned at a very early age to poke fun at myself and get a laugh before anyone else could. I now realize that was a common coping technique. That is why I became the "funny fat friend". I had already given myself that label.

When it came to sports I was coordinated – but it HURT because I was fat. So I convinced myself that I didn't like to play sports. My parents recognized this and still made me play, but by the time I got into high school I had worn them down. Finally, in the spring of my freshman year I broke my foot during football practice and stopped playing team sports. I did play one season on the tennis team, but I was a senior and it was with my friends.

I left a few weeks after high school to attend university at Brigham Young University and things stayed the same for me physically. I attended for 1 year and then left to go on a mission to the Spain Las Palmas Mission in the Canary Islands, where I experienced two of the best and most difficult years of my life. On my mission, I changed as a person in regards to maturity and the direction my life was headed. Focusing on Christ during those 2 years made me healthier spiritually and physically. It helped that my mission was a walking mission, I walked (or rode the bus) everywhere. There was even a point near the end of my mission that I would rise early in the mornings with my companion and we would go for a run. This was my first experience (albeit for only a few weeks) that I ever ran. I came home from my mission at my lightest weight I had ever been, about 220 lbs. I remember setting a conscious goal to come home from my mission a thinner man, and I loved shocking my mom as I walked off the plane.

I was also motivated by "love." Before I left on my mission I grew close to a girl that I had been "in love" with for much of my high school career. Sadly, she never felt the same about me. I was always just her close friend. At one point she even dated my brother. I knew the reason she never felt the same for me was because of my size. This was confirmed weeks before my mission when she told me that if I came home from my mission having lost a lot of weight, she would be there for me. I thought that was great and I was motivated. The sad thing is I wasn't even out of the Missionary Training Center before she had found another guy and was in a serious relationship. I always worried that I would never find anyone that would love me for me. This plagued me to a point in my life where I developed low self-esteem and confidence issues. I always fell back to the "fat funny guy" persona.

After my mission I came home and was involved in a young single adult group. That's where I first saw Melanie. As I was walking into a building she was outside. She was dressed all in black wearing a sweat shirt and stretchy pants and I thought to myself, "Holy crap, she is hot!" I don't think she noticed me at all.

It must have been a couple weeks later that I was driving home from my warehouse job in Tigard when I passed her on the commute home. I remember looking over at the car next to me and recognizing her. For some reason I started waving frantically like a crazy person. I have no idea what came over me. It felt like I was having an out of body experience and I'm sure it left an impression on her. As she stared back at me in horror, I realized that she had no idea who I was, and I sped away as fast as I could. The next Sunday when I saw her at church she definitely recognized me. We had a short introduction, and I'm sure I was awkward and tried to make some silly joke. At least I had finally talked to her. At this point, I had started gaining back my weight and had put on about 30 lbs.

A few weeks later there was a Christmas party for the young single adults and it was held at my parents' house because I was in charge of organizing the event. Melanie was there and I spent the entire party "following" her around, although I would like to think that I was a little covert with my actions. That night was a very difficult one for Melanie because it was the anniversary of her previous marriage and her ex was there with his current girlfriend, which made for an uncomfortable situation. Ultimately, this played well in my favor. The next day she called to thank me for hosting the party and asked me to go Christmas tree shopping with her! That was our first date. The next 2 weeks we spent time together everyday and I fell fast in love with her.

One night I was leaving her house to go home and desperately wanted to give her a goodnight kiss, but I could tell that she was reluctant. I had the distinct impression that she was hesitant because I was fat. So in true Trent fashion I asked her "it's because I'm fat, isn't it?" and it was! With this out in the open and my greatest fears and vulnerability splayed out on the table – we did have our first kiss, and boy let me tell you, the heavens opened and the fireworks exploded and I knocked her socks off. Let's just say, it was a great first kiss.

A couple weeks later I left to head back to Utah and start BYU again. Over the next 3 months, I flew home twice and had flown her down once to see me. We were in love, then engaged, and married on May 14th, 1994. I share this brief explanation of our courtship and marriage because its fun and I love my wife with all my heart. She is an integral part of my life. I have no secrets from her. The next 18 years happened, life is hard – kids, illness, work, homes, school, job losses, businesses, bankruptcy, and many many more trials and blessings which brought me to my journey of change.

I want to make sure that you, the reader, know that you have the power within to change your life for the better, to confront that which holds you back, and know that all this comes from realizing your potential. I pose the question, "Where does that power come from?" The answer is Jesus Christ. Learning, following, and loving Him. This kind of transformation will be unlike anything you thought possible. Moroni, in the Book of Mormon, says "All things which are good cometh of God." This I know to be true. Now let the journey begin.

CHAPTER 1
The Goal

MY JOURNEY STARTED 6 years ago when I was 35 and had a crazy goal. My life was in a bit of turmoil, I had a lot of business and personal things happening. Somehow in the middle of it all I thought to myself that I needed to do something incredible, something that made me reach for the stars, and something that would not be easy for me to accomplish. Now as I look back, I realize it was inspired for me to reach for such a dream.

I decided I would run a marathon by the time I was 40! Why a marathon? It is something that most people are familiar with. A marathon is something that most can't or won't ever do, yet it's humanly possible, so it would make me special for doing it. Let me make something very clear however – I AM NOT A RUNNER, as a matter a fact I ALWAYS HATED RUNNING. What the crud was I thinking? Regardless, I put some thought into this goal of running a marathon and pondered it over many days. Eventually I committed to it.

One of the other reasons that I chose to run a marathon was because my brother is an Ironman triathlete and at that time in his life he was fully engulfed in training for his races as he attempted to qualify for the championship race in Kona, HI. It was great to see him succeed at this and see the attention and growth he was getting from it. Not only was he an example of the commitment that was needed to do this kind of race, but on a much deeper level, I had always idolized my brother. When we were young, I was the pesky little brother following him and his friends around. I have always desperately wanted to be close to him and I hoped that completing a marathon would show him that I was worthy of his time and attention. My relationship with my brother has been strained at best and contemptuous at worst. This has been one of the greatest struggles in my life up until I finished my marathon. I will share more of my relationship with my brother later.

I chose a marathon over a triathlon because everyone

knows a marathon is 26.2 miles, but a triathlon can be many distances. There are sprint, olympic, half, and full Ironman distances, but nobody *really* knows what that entails except for triathletes themselves. There is also more equipment and training required to do a triathlon since you swim, cycle, and run.

By carrying out this goal I believed it would be the solution to finally getting my weight under control and not being fat. Looking back, I can't emphasize enough the importance of setting a goal like this. The crazy thing is the difference between what I did about this goal 6 years ago and what I did the year prior to my marathon. 6 years ago I did exactly one thing – I told one person about my goal and desire to run a marathon. I told my best friend and brother-in-law, Mike. I didn't even tell Melanie. Mike has been a runner all his life. He was the high school cross country and track coach and he ran almost every day. I guess I thought that by telling him I would be motivated to actually do something about reaching my goal. I hoped that Mike would give me the "magic running pill" and I would all of a sudden love running and knock this marathon thing out. Well that didn't happen and that pill doesn't exist.

5 years passed and though I never forgot about the

marathon goal – I didn't do anything to accomplish it. Periodically I would think about it and the thought would come "Oh, I only have 3 years now to train for the marathon." But, I never did anything about it. Setting a goal is imperative, necessary, a must do. However, if you don't do anything about it, it's just a nice idea. That's what I had those first 5 years – just a nice idea.

CHAPTER 2
Turning 40

WHEN I WAS between the ages of 35-40 my family moved to Vancouver, WA. In our new church's Ward (congregation) I was serving in the young mens' program with Scott Gifford and Ty Engstrom. Scott and Ty were always talking about their next workout together, and the next race coming up, and the new gizmo they got for their bike, and so on… I was the odd (fat) man out. I didn't understand half of the things they were talking about. I envied their friendship. I really liked these guys and I wanted to be like them.

The day before my 40th birthday we were at a ward BBQ. It was a typical BBQ, hamburgers and hot dogs. I'm sure I ate 2 of each with plenty of side dishes. After I had eaten, I was milling around with Mel, and I was in a pretty deep funk. The goal I had set all those years ago was very prevalent in my thoughts. I was struck on a very deep level with a question about who I was. In my mind all I could think was – "Am I that loser, that imbecile, that poser that sets a goal for himself and then does nothing?" I mean how could I have done absolutely nothing about it? These thoughts fairly well consumed me that night.

Later that night, with Mel by my side, I found myself standing behind Scott. He was talking to someone else with his back to me. As I stood there for a few moments with no one to talk to, and no one wanting to talk to me, the thought occurred, "Ask Scott to be your personal trainer." I immediately suppressed that thought – shoved it back where it came from, but it came again, and I started getting scared. I was afraid he would say, "Yes." I was afraid he would say, "No." I was afraid he would laugh, or ignore me, or I didn't know… I was afraid of everything. Without realizing what was happening, and almost without my own will, I heard myself asking Mel if I should ask Scott to be my personal trainer. She very enthusiastically agreed that this was a great idea and I turned and said, "Scott, will you be my personal trainer?" Then in classic

Scott fashion he turned around slowly, looked me straight in the eye and said, "Yes." BAM – right there it started. The die had been cast, and something major shifted. That was a very powerful moment. I, however, in typical Trent fashion, tried to brush it off. That didn't last long and Scott asked me a couple questions and said that he would set up a time to come over and talk about it. After the conversation, I tried to ignore that it had happened, but deep in my spirit, my soul, my psyche, I knew something had changed. Something felt different.

That next weekend was great and calorie filled with my favorite pizza and cake to celebrate my 40th birthday. To top it off there was a surprise party with family and friends. I thoroughly over indulged and loved every minute of it. I look back at the beginning of my journey and recognize the importance of all the memories. And my enjoyment of turning 40 is one of them. It felt fitting that it started with TONS of calories!

The memory of asking Scott makes me realize that that is when the ball had been set in motion. In that instant, when those 7 words came out of my mouth, the plan that Heavenly Father had in store for me began. It was nothing like I expected or what I thought was in the realm of possibility for me.

CHAPTER 3
The Plan

MY LIFE HAS always has been about "the plan." Mel use to joke with me early in our marriage about "the plan," whether it was cars, kids, food, anything. It was all a part of "the plan." For me a plan is vital, and for this journey here is the way the plan went down.

It was a Tuesday night, 5 days after my birthday when Scott and Ty came over to lay out my plan. Scott told me that he felt like Ty should be involved in the process and had asked him to come meet with me. I am very grateful that he did and whole heartedly agreed. It felt like the right team. I thought, "Maybe now I won't be the odd man out."

One of the most important things in my journey

happened a few days prior to this meeting. Scott gave me the book "He Did Deliver Me from Bondage" by Colleen C. Harrison as a birthday present. He told me that he had an acquaintance that had recently lost a lot of weight. When he asked her what *one* thing made the biggest difference, she told him it was this book, so Scott bought a copy and gave it to me.

The meeting lasted a couple hours with my wife Mel and our 2 kids Jonaka and Beyden. Jonaka's friend was also over that night. The first half hour we discussed my history, particularly with food, dieting, and where I had been with my weight. We talked about lifestyle, barriers in the past, and why I wanted to change now. Scott showed up with a self-made outline that he took notes on. I kept the outline after that evening and it became a guide and a check in sheet during my journey. I taped it on the inside cover of my journal. This is the sheet now, all filled out:

332.4 – TRENTS WEIGHT ON 8/28/12 @ 9:45 PM L/C
215.0 – TRENTS WEIGHT ON 12/01/12 @ 8:15 AM SG
235.8 – TRENTS WEIGHT ON 3/1/13 @ 6:05 AM –SG
203.4 – TRENTS WEIGHT ON 6/1/13 @ SG 5:15 8/28/2012
194.2 – TRENTS WEIGHT ON 8/24/13 @ 7:25 AM SG

Trent Heppler 2012

Goals   MARATHON 2013

– FRIENDSHIPS   COUNTRY GATOR GRINDER
                                         REALISTIC   STRETCH   MAY
– LOSE WEIGHT ≥ 335   220   175

– SUSTAINABILITY FOOD

How hard do you want to push it?   THE – WED 8:30 TO 5PM
                                          THUR 6:30 TO 3:30 GENDEN GYM
    2000 CALORIES –   MON + FRI, OM, SAT
                                         5 OUT OF 10 RAIN
TY – BIKE NEEDS TUNE UP
    – RECUMBENT   – 6 DAYS OF CARDIO
SCOTT – SHOES   – MON, TUE MIN
Accountability
– 3 MONTH BLOCKS, 4 ANSWERS

– 1x WEEK TUE   FINAL WEIGH
                                                            AUG 23RD
Dec 1: 275   MARCH 1: 210   JUNE 1: 215   195 194.2
    57.4 LBS   @   25   20   Celebrate breakfast
Support   w/ Scott +
– MEDS 5-6/DAY   – MYFITNESSPAL.com – ONLINE COUNTING   Britt Heavy TY.
– "ARE YOU SURE YOU WANT TO DO THAT?" – MELANIE ONLY
– TY + SCOTT TEXTING

Diet
– NO SWEETS
– BE OPEN FOOD IN FRONT OF DAD

Exercise Plan
40 MIN CARDIO + TEXTING

800 – 823 – 2000
medical Reports – David
July 15th 2010 322 Lbs
per
KP   march 2010 340 lbs.
                    Highest

The details of the outline and my plan are on that sheet. One of the first questions that Scott asked me was, "What are your goals?" These are the ones that we set that night.

1. I wanted a friendship with Scott and Ty. (To which Scott replied, "That's a given.")

2. To lose weight. (I told him I was ± 335 lbs and wanted to set a realistic weight loss goal down to 220 lbs. with a stretch goal of 195 lbs.)

3. To finish a marathon by the time I was 40, meaning before I turned 41 on my next birthday. (Both Scott and Ty are triathletes and wanted me to do a triathlon, but after my explanation of the marathon preference, they understood and supported my goal 100%.)

4. To have sustainability – to maintain and continue on the journey and not quit.

5. To learn what food to eat, how much of it and what to do when I got hungry.

Scott then asked me how hard I wanted to push it and we discussed some of the details surrounding that. These details were:

1. We reviewed my work schedule and figured out when it was appropriate for me to exercise.

2. I would eat less than 2000 calories a day to begin with.

3. I would do cardio for 6 days a week, Monday through Saturday, taking Sunday off.

4. Since I didn't have any shoes that were adequate to walk in, Ty would give me two pairs of his old running shoes (luckily we are the same size). They worked great.

5. I would do a combination of walking and riding the recumbent stationary bike, which I had bought years earlier and had recently become a clothes hanger.

We then talked about accountability. This is one of the keys to success in my journey. Having someone to hold me accountable was SUPER important. These are the items we set up for accountability:

1. I would have 4 official weigh-ins, 3 months apart. Every quarter we would meet together to get on the scale.

   - The starting weigh-in was the night of our first meeting.
   - The first was scheduled for 12-1-2012 with a goal weight of 275 lbs.
   - The second was scheduled for 3-1-2013 with a goal weight of 240 lbs.
   - The third was scheduled for 6-1-2013 with a goal weight of 215 lbs.
   - The fourth and final weigh-in was scheduled for 8-23-2013 (my 41st Birthday) with my stretch goal weight of 195 lbs.

2. I would weigh myself every week during my journey, the same day of the week, first thing in the morning, after I had gone to the bathroom and without clothing.

Next on the outline was to discuss support and the details of the expectations for me, my family, Scott and Ty.

1. I would eat 5-6 small meals a day, eating a few hours apart. These meals would be smaller in portion and more frequent. (I was really worried about this change).

2. I would count all my calories. Everything that crossed my lips I would log into MyFitnessPal.com - an online health and fitness website and forum. Melanie got online and set up an account for me that night.

3. I would text Scott and Ty EVERY night with my calories eaten for the day and what exercise I had completed.

That evening we briefly discussed the foods I was going to eat. There was no discussion of eating super healthy, just that I needed to cut out sweets and stay under my 2,000 calorie limit each day. We also talked with Beyden because I was concerned that it would be really difficult for me to watch him eat. He is a football player and eats as I used too and it scared me that I would not be able to partake myself in the same manner. We agreed that he would consume these large amounts of food away from me, particularly in the evenings when I knew my hunger pains would be the greatest.

The next area on the outline was the exercise plan. This was pretty simple, 40 minutes a day, 6 days a week with the text to Scott and Ty nightly stating what I had completed.

Here is the video of me doing my starting weigh-in. This is the link and QR code you can scan to watch it: http://bit.ly/powerwithin1

My official starting weight was 332.4 lbs. However, I had contacted my previous medical clinic and asked them what my highest recorded weight was and they told me that in March of 2010 I weighed in at 340 lbs. I believe at my heaviest I was easily between 350-360 lbs. I, like most fat people, wasn't weighing myself on a regular (if ever) basis. We then took beginning measurements of my right arm, shoulders, chest, abdomen, and right leg. These are shared in the end of the book to show my progression.

Here are some before pictures:

After the meeting, Beyden told me to write in my journal, so I found a notebook and for the first time in decades, I wrote. Throughout my journey I have written in it. Sometimes daily and other times less regularly, but it has been a very important part of the process. I have carried it with me nearly everywhere I have gone over the last year. That same journal is where I taped the outline from our first meeting. I use many quotes from this journal and refer to it often in this book.

This is a quote from my very first journal entry that night on August 28th, 2013:

"I don't know what to write. I've just started a program with Scott Gifford and Ty Engstrom to change my life and my son told me to write in my journal, so I am. I'm nervous I'll start and not finish, but I also think now more than ever with this support I will succeed. I have this weird thing that if I write this down I will be less likely to accomplish it. However right now I don't believe that. The meeting tonight with Scott and Ty, and my family was very good, almost 2 hours full of the spirit and support for me. I also feel the book I'm reading can really change my life. Scott gave it to me."

And we were off…

CHAPTER 4

Food... and Addictions

MY FIRST GOAL was to lose 57.4 lbs and go from 332.4 lbs to 275 lbs within 3 months. Right after the meeting with Scott and Ty I was filled with the initial excitement, momentum, and a good attitude. It didn't take long for that to wear off. In my case it was a couple of weeks. I wrote in my journal two weeks after I had started the process that the initial excitement had worn off and now it was just work. For those of you that make New Years resolutions, you know what I mean. It was time to get down to real work. I had to remember the basics.

Basic #1 – eat less than 2000 calories a day. This required counting calories. I had never done that before and as a matter a fact, I always thought it was ridiculous.

All those people that were consumed by counting calories were impractical. But then it happened to me and because of the "laws of life", I became the exact thing that used to annoy me. I was consumed with counting calories!

That very next day after my first meeting I started logging everything I ate into the MyFitnessPal.com (MFP) website. Soon this became my newest addiction. Interestingly enough the first week of logging, my family left for the weekend to go on our annual camping trip for Labor Day weekend and I was unable to enter my calories. So, I wrote everything I ate in my journal to be entered later. Around this time in the beginning I wasn't so concerned with the exact types of food I was eating, I just cared about eating less than 2000 calories. The only thing I tried to do was stay away from sweets to reduce my carbs. Here is an example of my food intake in the beginning. It is 3 consecutive days in September 2012:

September 10, 2012

Foods	Calories	Carbs	Fat	Protein	Cholest	Sodium	Sugars	Fiber
Breakfast								
Milk - Reduced fat, 2%	122	11g	5g	8g	20mg	100mg	12g	0g
Millville - Oats and	240	38g	8g	5g	0mg	100mg	13g	4g
Snack am								
Watermelon - Raw, 2	92	23g	0g	2g	0mg	3mg	19g	1g
Cheese - Cheddar, 1.5	169	1g	14g	10g	44mg	261mg	0g	0g
Generic - Kraft Free	15	3g	0g	0g	0mg	480mg	2g	0g
Carrots - Baby, raw, 3	16	4g	0g	0g	0mg	35mg	2g	1g
Broccoli - Flower	15	3g	0g	2g	0mg	14mg	0g	0g
Lettuce - Iceberg	16	3g	0g	1g	0mg	12mg	2g	1g
Ham - Sliced, regular	91	2g	5g	9g	32mg	730mg	0g	1g
Fresh - Tomatoes on	3	1g	0g	0g	0mg	1mg	1g	0g
Mushrooms - Raw,	2	0g	0g	0g	0mg	0mg	0g	0g
Lunch								
Homemade - Salisbury	295	0g	21g	24g	0mg	0mg	0g	0g
Generic - Mashed	120	11g	0g	0g	0mg	0mg	0g	0g
Broccoli - Steamed	50	8g	0g	6g	0mg	50mg	0g	6g
Generic - Yellow	93	5g	8g	0g	0mg	8mg	0g	0g

Snacks pm

Butter - Salted, 2 pat	72	0g	8g	0g	22mg	58mg	0g	0g
Orowheat - Health Full	160	32g	2g	10g	0mg	300mg	4g	10g
Fried Egg - 2 Eggs	140	1g	11g	13g	422mg	278mg	1g	0g
Chachies - Mango	50	12g	0g	0g	0mg	170mg	6g	0g
Snacks - Tortilla chips,	284	36g	15g	4g	0mg	299mg	0g	4g
TOTAL:	2,045	194g	97g	94g	540mg	2,899mg	62g	28g

September 11, 2012

Foods	Calories	Carbs	Fat	Protein	Cholest	Sodium	Sugars	Fiber

Breakfast

Milk - Reduced	122	11g	5g	8g	20mg	100mg	12g	0g
Millville - Oats	240	38g	8g	5g	0mg	100mg	13g	4g

Snack am

Homemade -	295	0g	21g	24g	0mg	0mg	0g	0g
Generic -	120	11g	0g	0g	0mg	0mg	0g	0g
Broccoli -	25	4g	0g	3g	0mg	25mg	0g	3g
Generic - Yellow	93	5g	8g	0g	0mg	8mg	0g	0g

Lunch

Generic - Yellow	37	2g	3g	0g	0mg	3mg	0g	0g
Cheese -	113	0g	9g	7g	29mg	174mg	0g	0g

Foods	Calories	Carbs	Fat	Protein	Cholest	Sodium	Sugars	Fiber
Mushrooms -	8	1g	0g	1g	0mg	1mg	1g	0g
Fried Egg - 2	210	1g	16g	19g	633mg	417mg	1g	0g
Generic - 2	70	0g	6g	4g	30mg	360mg	0g	0g
Butter - Salted, 1	36	0g	4g	0g	11mg	29mg	0g	0g
Bread - Whole-	69	13g	1g	3g	0mg	148mg	6g	2g

Snacks pm

Foods	Calories	Carbs	Fat	Protein	Cholest	Sodium	Sugars	Fiber
Cheese -	113	0g	9g	7g	29mg	174mg	0g	0g
Fruit - Orange, 1	62	15g	0g	1g	0mg	0mg	12g	3g
Fresh Fruit -	110	29g	0g	1g	0mg	3mg	25g	1g
General Mills -	170	20g	9g	4g	0mg	140mg	12g	2g
TOTAL:	1,893	150g	99g	87g	752mg	1,682mg	82g	15g

September 12, 2012

Foods	Calories	Carbs	Fat	Protein	Cholest	Sodium	Sugars	Fiber

Breakfast

Foods	Calories	Carbs	Fat	Protein	Cholest	Sodium	Sugars	Fiber
Butter - Salted, 2	72	0g	8g	0g	22mg	58mg	0g	0g
Bread - Whole-	139	26g	2g	5g	0mg	296mg	11g	4g
Fried Egg - 2	140	1g	11g	13g	422mg	278mg	1g	0g

Foods	Calories	Carbs	Fat	Protein	Cholest	Sodium	Sugars	Fiber
Snack am								
Cheese -	85	0g	7g	5g	22mg	130mg	0g	0g
Bars/Franz -	290	22g	17g	11g	35mg	890mg	0g	0g
Lunch								
Homemade -	191	10g	3g	30g	78mg	1,135mg	0g	3g
Homemade: -	360	74g	2g	18g	0mg	20mg	4g	2g
Snacks pm								
Generic - Nature	190	29g	6g	4g	0mg	160mg	12g	2g
Bananas - Raw,	105	27g	0g	1g	0mg	1mg	14g	3g
Fruit - Orange, 1	62	15g	0g	1g	0mg	0mg	12g	3g
Bread - Banana,	69	12g	2g	1g	9mg	64mg	0g	0g
Homemade -	75	9g	7g	1g	10mg	42mg	6g	0g
TOTAL:	**1,778**	**225g**	**65g**	**90g**	**598mg**	**3,074mg**	**60g**	**17g**

As you can see I usually kept my calories around 2000 and I pretty quickly reduced that to 1900 within just a few weeks. I stayed true to this logging and intake for the first 3 months. I eventually reduced my calories to less than

1750 a day after a couple months.

What isn't clear from these tables is that I ate 5 to 6 meals a day. They were smaller meals between 200-400 calories each. A meal might be an apple and some carrots, or a peanut butter and jam sandwich. One of the primary reasons this was successful was because Mel would prepare 3 or 4 of these meals in the morning that I would take with me to work. I found it critical to my success that I wasn't the one preparing these meals, because my tendency was, and still is, to embellish them with extra calories of every sort, i.e. extra cheese, more mayo, a couple extra slices of meat etc. After a month or so, I found myself really looking forward to the food. I would think, "Oh great I have grapes and a tuna sandwich to eat!" and then my mouth would water for it. I did not settle for unhealthy food like I would have in the past. Eating that food would start the cravings for more unhealthy food like a pizza, a donut, or a quesadilla.

Since I was keeping to a schedule, it was possible for me to manage hunger pains. It was common that I would eat one of my meals and would still feel hungry. My eating schedule was something I relied on. Food and eating took on a whole new meaning. In the evenings, after I had finished my last meal, I would have moderate to severe hunger pains for the rest of the night. Yes, **every night**. I thought they would never go away. These pains lasted for months. They finally started to subside for me around month 7 or 8.

I would eat my first meal at 6:30am. This meal became very important to me because after I would wake up the hunger pains would be gone, but my system needed fuel to get it going. Before I started my journey I was one of those people that never ate breakfast. When I would, I could never finish it because it would start to taste bad to me. It was very weird. I would typically get quite hungry around 10:00 am and eat a *big* meal *before* lunch. Nowadays my breakfast is typically a ¼ to ½ cup granola or cereal, and ½ cup milk. Since this is such a small amount, I put it in a really small bowl to make it look like more food and feel more satisfying to me.

My other small meals would be at 9:30/10:00 am, then 12:30/1:00 pm, then 2:30/3:00 pm, and then typically my last meal was between 5:00 and 6:00 pm. In the beginning I didn't eat past 7:00pm at Ty's suggestion. I logged everything into the website and became a little obsessed, needing to make sure I got it done before I ate, or immediately after. I needed to know exactly where I was throughout the day. I much preferred to pre-log my food for a day, and then I wouldn't have to worry about what I was going to eat. When I first started logging on MFP, I didn't add any "pals" from the site. After using it for a month or so, I felt more comfortable with it and I started seeking and accepting friend requests. Over time MyFitness"Pals" became very important to me. They helped keep me accountable because they were reviewing my diary on a daily basis and commenting on my successes everyday. Some of my pals have become my greatest supporters and I can't wait to read their comments. I would also log my exercise in everyday and my weight every week.

This chapter should probably be titled, "Addictions to Food" except when I started I didn't believe that I had an addiction. I must have said dozens of times in my life when I was 350 lbs, "I don't eat more than most people. I have maintained this weight all my life." Well, I was delusional.

When I finally began to realize that I had an eating addiction, things got serious. It is a pretty surreal moment when you admit to yourself that you don't have control of something as basic as food and eating, but that it has control over you. I realize that throughout my life I would secretly snack and eat bites and meals in addition to all the "public" eating I would do. This was normal for me and I never saw it as a problem, as most people with an addiction tend to believe.

The book that Scott gave me, "He Did Deliver Me from Bondage" is based on the 12 steps of the Alcoholics Anonymous program. It uses the principles of the Gospel of Jesus Christ and scripture from the Book of Mormon to support each principle. When Scott gave me the book, I read the description and I thought to myself, "I'm not doing the AA 12 step program." Then I started to read it. I've never been a reader, but this book spoke to me and hit a nerve. I read pretty much everyday. The first time I read it, I did so like it was a novel. I didn't institute the principles or do the suggested actions in the book, but I could feel it having a profound effect on me. I was changing.

The 12 steps are powerful and I share them here as they are written in Colleen C. Harrison's book "He Did Deliver Me from Bondage." This is simply a list to give you an idea of the steps and progression of addressing an addiction. I encourage you to study the book and apply the steps for yourself. It will be life changing.

1. I of myself am powerless – nothing without God.

2. All power of redemption and atonement is vested in the Lord Jesus Christ, and this power can only be effective in my life as I am willing to have a personal relationship with Him.

3. Trusting God in all things is the highest form of worship I can extend to him.

4. My trials and mistakes are potentially great learning opportunities, not terrible things I should try to ignore or forget.

5. I must be willing to tell the whole truth to another person about my weaknesses and failings when I am moved by the Spirit of the Lord to do so.

6. Only a mighty change in my heart, a complete change of disposition, of desire, will ensure any genuine change in my behavior.

7. The mighty change of heart is a gift from God that I must desire and ask for.

8. The mighty change of heart brings a willingness to

make amends for all the past wrongs, to seek a spirit of peace and oneness with everyone, including those I have hurt or been hurt by.

9. The establishment of Zion begins with a mighty change in my own heart and then extends to others as I act to amend all past wrongs.

10. The mighty change of heart does not bring me to a state of perfection but rather to a state of continual repentance and abhorrence of sin.

11. The mighty change of heart brings me an awareness of Christ's living presence in my life through the gift of the Holy Ghost as I learn to receive and believe the voice of the Lord in my own mind.

12. The experience of being born again, of being changed from the inside out, causes two spontaneous reactions in me: (1) an irrepressible desire to share with others the good news of God's reality and availability, and (2) an ever-increasing willingness to practice these principles in every area of my life.

I truly started to realize, while reading the book, that none of the changes I needed to make would be possible except through Christ. I had to understand that Christ is the higher power and the "power within" only comes from Him. Without comprehending it, my whole being began to change, not just my body. One lesson I learned was on a walk one day during lunch break. It was a thought that came to me and I was impressed to write it down. It was, "In the Lords work there is not time for TV, video games, or overeating, etc..." I have often thought back on this as I continue to fight my addictions with food and couch potatory (I think I just made a new word). I've never been a gamer but it struck me that any addiction, including those to video games, sports, soda, or seeking the worlds' praises, all remove you from that which the Lord would have you do and be. I believe everyone has some kind of addiction in their life that draws them away from doing the Lords work. Many don't know it and can't see it, just as I couldn't – but they exist!

As I read from this book, and from my patriarchal blessing, wonderful changes occurred in my life. One month after starting the journey on September 30th, 2012, I read step 6 in the book and I wrote this in my journal:

"I agreed to my trials and challenges before coming to earth. I did it gladly to participate in Christ's plan and now that I have them I wallow and moan and don't move on well. NO VICTIM. I will choose to release my weights that confine my soul, I will choose to be an example, to love, judge in righteousness — not like I have. Be the person God knows I am."

CHAPTER 5
Walking

THE EXERCISE I did for the first 3 months of my journey was primarily walking. Out of those 3 months I exercised 82 days, and 65 of those days involved walking. These periods of exercise transformed quickly from just a physical benefit to a benefit towards my body, mind, and spirit. It seems as though when something is good for your health, it's good for your whole being.

In the beginning it hurt my knees, my joints, my back, all of it – but I eventually got stronger and I learned how to push through the pain, and not let it stop me. I remember there were a couple of weeks where, after the first 10 minutes, I would get terrible shin splints and it made me want to stop so badly. But I didn't. Eventually my shin splints stopped hurting, but something else almost always took its place. This was one of the main things that kept me from continuing any kind of exercise regimen in the past. Scott had asked me before what my pain tolerance was and I knew it was low. I had proved that many times in the past 2 decades. I was glad this time I wasn't letting that stop me.

I would listen to music as I exercised. I started out with the contemporary music I had on my phone. I found that it kept my mind on the things of the world and that's not where I wanted it to be. So I quickly altered the use of time during exercise to meditate, think, and pray.

Just a couple of weeks into my journey, Mel was down in Portland trying out for the Portland Ensign Choir and Orchestra (PECO). It's a choral and orchestra group that does 2 or 3 excellent concerts a year with fantastic performers. While she was there I got a phone call and she told me that her audition had gone very well and would likely be accepted into the choir, but that if she was able to bring a male voice with her (especially a tenor), her chances of acceptance would be improved. So I jumped in my car and arrived at the auditions within 30 minutes. I hadn't prepared a song, but made it through the auditions without sounding too bad. We stayed that night for practice and a week later were asked to join the choir. Being members of the choir has been a wonderful blessing in our lives and another notable part of my journey.

After we joined the choir there was a lot of music memorizing to be done so I thought it would be smart to listen to the Christmas songs we were learning as I exercised. After I switched to the Christmas music, I started to view my walks as a spiritual time versus exercise time. This is when the idea of a healthy body and spirit started to tie together in my mind. Identifying exercise as a spiritual act has continued to this day. Most times I exercise I try to focus on spiritual influences by listening to PECO practice songs, scriptures, spiritual talks, and articles in the Ensign. I do this all while praying and meditating.

As I did this, I slowly started to notice changes in myself. I wrote in my journal on October 3rd, 2012:

"At work now, just got back from a walk and I'm eating grapes. I am getting to the point where I feel better when I'm exercising. I may be starting to look forward to it. I really am. I'm just afraid to say so, because then I will stop looking forward to it (knock on wood). Last night was PECO practice, I am really enjoying singing with Mel and this fantastic choir, I almost don't feel good enough, but I'm glad I'm there. I want to find where I fit in and who I can be

friends with. Mel told me yesterday that I seem to be less irritable or reclusive since I've been dieting and exercising, maybe I see a little of that as well (knock on wood). I really love my kids Jonni and Beyden; I also want to be in great shape."

I would go on many of my walks during my lunch break at work (instead of eating ☺) and this also became a time of renewal from the stresses of my job. I would go sun, rain, or snow. There were more than a couple times I came back soaking wet or sweaty. Eventually I got it all figured out and would make sure I had an umbrella and at least a change of shirt depending on the conditions.

As I read the book, exercised, and felt the spirit more, I wanted more of those things. My weight loss journey became one of transformation because I was seeking after the good. A pathway was set and a foundation was being built. This is what I wanted – a renewed life in body, mind, and spirit. I was starting to get a glimpse of the connection between a healthy body and spirit. I was changing. But remember, although change is good – IT'S NOT EASY!

CHAPTER 6
Weigh-in #1

DECEMBER 1ST 2012 was the date of my first weigh-in, and I was nervous. I was supposed to have lost 57.4 lbs and I didn't know if I had done it. By then I had had time to grasp an understanding of the nature of weight loss. Even though I knew I was supposed to weigh myself only once a week I couldn't help but step on the scale every morning. I think this is something that many struggle with. What that did for me was help me understand the cyclical nature of weight loss and get a better understanding of how my body works. There are days when you lose no weight, and days where you gain weight, and then days when you lose 4 pounds. I came to realize that my body was on a 2 to 4 day cycle, so what I ate yesterday didn't really matter. It was what I ate and how I exercised 2, 3, or 4 days ago that made the difference. I think this is where so many people get frustrated. Let's say you get back from a great walk, keep the calories down, make great choices, fight the hunger pains, and keep the inner demons from escaping. But once you step on the scale it says you have gained a pound and it ticks the heck out of you. Well that is weight loss! You have to persist.

I've also come to understand that visualization is a big part of changing anything in your life. Close your eyes and imagine where and who you want to be in a month from now, then in 6 months from now, and do that everyday. If you do this it will allow you to make it happen. Visualizing success of any kind - losing weight, completing a walk, shooting a basket, winning that competition, making a change in your life in whatever form - is POWERFUL.

When I weighed myself I would do it in the morning after I had gone to the restroom and without any clothes on. I found this is when I was at my lightest. It's not important when you weigh yourself, it's only important that you are consistently doing it at the same time and under the same conditions to get an accurate result. Just for reinforcement, I would record my weight loss every week on MyFitnessPal.

On December 1st 2012 Scott came over first thing in the morning, since that was the time I normally weighed myself, but this morning it would be for my first official weigh-in. He videoed all of the weigh-ins on his phone. Here is the link and QR code for scanning to view the video. http://bit.ly/powerwithin2

That was a pretty exciting moment for me as I stepped on that scale; I did not know if I would make my goal. But as the scale flipped back and forth from 274 to 275 and finally stopped on 275 I was super happy. First major hurdle cleared! I was ecstatic that I met my goal. It was a stepping stone in my larger goal to running a marathon. And I DID IT!

Each accomplished goal was rewarded, and the first reward was a couple weeks later. Scott, Ty, and I met and went bowling. I'm pretty sure I won – which doesn't really matter except for the fact that all 3 of us are super competitive, and since I can't (yet!) beat them in a race, I need the whole world to know I beat them at bowling! We were all becoming friends and I was very happy about that, it was one of the things that was most important to me. I can't express my thanks enough for the support, accountability, and positive feedback I got from Scott and Ty throughout my journey.

On December 2, 2012 I wrote in my journal:

"Yesterday was my 1st quarter official weigh-in. My goal was 275 lbs. Scott came over and I weighed exactly 275.0 lbs. It felt great, I am glad I met my goal. There are a lot of things that helped contribute to the success. Writing in this journal is one, reading the book, my wife's support in preparing my food is huge, and Scott and Ty and their example and accountability. I am very thankful for all those things."

CHAPTER 7
The Schedule/Calendar

I KNEW I needed to start running, but I had no idea where to begin. I eventually figured out a plan and scheduled out a workout calendar. I really like a plan. I have found it is necessary to schedule, plan, and write out my goals. That way it's more than just an idea – actions have to be taken.

On November 19th, 2012 I ran for the very first time. I didn't know what I was doing, but I wanted to start. I knew I needed to do interval running because that's what Ty told me. So my first run was walking 4 minutes and running 2 minutes. I did 8 reps of that, and I was worn out. Running is very different from walking; it's a much heavier cardio and strain on the body. 3 days later I ran again using the same interval. This time for 11 repetitions.

It was at this point that I started to research Jeff Galloway's website www.jeffgalloway.com. He wrote a book titled: "Marathon: You Can Do It!" that Ty had read when he was preparing for one of his previous marathons. Jeff is a proponent of the run/walk method of training/racing.

I had run a couple of times now, but I was no runner and the registration for the Foot Traffic Flat Marathon was coming up on December 3rd, 2012. I had been talking to Scott and Ty about it for a few weeks and I hadn't even really started running, so I was very scared. Saying I wanted to run a marathon and actually spending money to register for one are completely different things. I was second guessing the decision; I mean what was I thinking?? Before the registration opened I had only run 6 times for very few minutes each, and I was going to spend actual money, $90 to race a marathon?

It's worth explaining that throughout this entire journey I have either been unemployed, or underemployed, with no discretionary income. So spending the money was a big deal. I also had no health insurance which meant zero medical visits throughout this entire journey. This was the reality of my situation. It is certainly not something I would recommend, so please if you have the wherewithal to get medical advice, do so before and during your journey. In that sense it is helpful to be gainfully employed and with health coverage, but I didn't let that stop me.

So the morning of December 3rd I got up very early, around 5am, and signed up for the full marathon and paid my fee. That same morning Scott, Mike, and Ty's wife Holly also signed up. My number was 2041, so I think I was the 41st person to sign up for the full marathon. After I signed up I was excited and nervous (as I have been many many times throughout this journey) – but there was no turning back now. I couldn't get a refund. I had spent the money (that we didn't have), and I was going to run a marathon for real. At the computer that morning, my commitment deepened a little more. As my training progressed it continued to deepen with every step; physically, emotionally, and mentally.

A couple weeks later I created a calendar utilizing Jeff Galloway's template for finishing a marathon. I really like Jeff Galloway's interval method of training and racing, and think it was one of the keys that kept me from having any *serious* injury. Part of his program determines what your interval should be and he calls it the magic mile (mm). That is basically how fast you can run a mile after a warm up, then pushing yourself to run as hard as you can for a mile without puking. I did his online weekly workouts designed for marathon training and customized it to my specific dates and needs. I started the calendar on December 16th, 2012 and ended it on the date of the marathon, Independence Day, July 4th, 2013. I thought it was pretty cool that the marathon would coincide with Independence Day! Here is what the calendar looked like when I created it: it may be a little hard to read, but if you get out your magnifying glass, you shouldn't have any problems.

December 16, 2013 - July 4, 2013

	Sunday	Monday	Tuesday	Wednesday	Thursday	Friday	Saturday
Week 1	16 Dec. 2012 OFF	17 Intvrl: 30 MINUTE RUN Results:	18 EASY WALK Results:	19 Intvrl: 30 MINUTE RUN Results:	20 EASY WALK Results:	21 OFF	22 Intvrl: 4 MILES Results:
Week 2	23 OFF	24 Intvrl: 30 MINUTE RUN Results:	25 Christmas Day EASY WALK Results:	26 Intvrl: 30 MINUTE RUN Results:	27 EASY WALK Results:	28 OFF	29 Intvrl: 5 MILES Results:
Week 3	30 OFF	31 Intvrl: 30 MINUTE RUN Results:	1 January 2013 New Year's Day EASY WALK Results:	2 Intvrl: 30 MINUTE RUN Results:	3 EASY WALK Results:	4 OFF	5 Intvrl: 2.5 MILES / MM Results:
Week 4	6 OFF	7 Intvrl: 30 MINUTE RUN Results:	8 EASY WALK Results:	9 Intvrl: 30 MINUTE RUN Results:	10 EASY WALK Results:	11 OFF	12 Intvrl: 6 MILES Results:
Week 5	13 OFF	14 Beyonce Birthday Intvrl: 30 MINUTE RUN Results:	15 EASY WALK Results:	16 Intvrl: 30 MINUTE RUN Results:	17 EASY WALK Results:	18 OFF	19 Intvrl: 3 MILES Results:
Week 6	20 OFF	21 Martin Luther King Day Intvrl: 30 MINUTE RUN Results:	22 EASY WALK Results:	23 Intvrl: 30 MINUTE RUN Results:	24 EASY WALK Results:	25 OFF	26 Intvrl: 7.5 MILES Results:
Week 7	27 OFF	28 Intvrl: 30 MINUTE RUN Results:	29 EASY WALK Results:	30 Intvrl: 30 MINUTE RUN Results:	31 EASY WALK Results:	1 February 2013 OFF	2 Intvrl: 3 MILES / MM Results:
Week 8	3 OFF	4 Intvrl: 30 MINUTE RUN Results:	5 EASY WALK Results:	6 Intvrl: 30 MINUTE RUN Results:	7 EASY WALK Results:	8 OFF	9 Intvrl: 9 MILES Results:
Week 9	10 OFF	11 Intvrl: 30 MINUTE RUN Results:	12 EASY WALK Results:	13 Ash Wednesday Intvrl: 30 MINUTE RUN Results:	14 Valentine's Day EASY WALK Results:	15 OFF	16 Intvrl: 4 MILES Results:
Week 10	17 OFF	18 Presidents' Day Intvrl: 30 MINUTE RUN Results:	19 EASY WALK Results:	20 Intvrl: 30 MINUTE RUN Results:	21 EASY WALK Results:	22 OFF	23 Intvrl: 10.5 MILES Results:
Week 11	24 OFF	25 Intvrl: 30 MINUTE RUN Results:	26 EASY WALK Results:	27 Intvrl: 30 MINUTE RUN Results:	28 EASY WALK Results:	1 March 2013 Goal Weight 240 lbs. OFF	2 Intvrl: 4 MILES / MM Results:
Week 12	3 OFF	4 Intvrl: 30 MINUTE RUN Results:	5 EASY WALK Results:	6 Intvrl: 30 MINUTE RUN Results:	7 EASY WALK Results:	8 OFF	9 Intvrl: 12 MILES Results:
Week 13	10 Daylight Savings Begins OFF	11 Intvrl: 30 MINUTE RUN Results:	12 EASY WALK Results:	13 Intvrl: 30 MINUTE RUN Results:	14 EASY WALK Results:	15 OFF	16 Intvrl: 4 MILES Results:
Week 14	17 St. Patrick's Day OFF	18 Intvrl: 30 MINUTE RUN Results:	19 EASY WALK Results:	20 First Day of Spring Intvrl: 30 MINUTE RUN Results:	21 EASY WALK Results:	22 OFF	23 Intvrl: 14 MILES Results:
Week 15	24 Palm Sunday OFF	25 Intvrl: 30 MINUTE RUN Results:	26 EASY WALK Results:	27 Intvrl: 30 MINUTE RUN Results:	28 EASY WALK Results:	29 Good Friday OFF	30 Intvrl: 5 MILES / MM Results:
Week 16	31 Easter OFF	1 April 2013 Janeka's Birthday 30 MINUTE RUN Results:	2 EASY WALK Results:	3 Intvrl: 30 MINUTE RUN Results:	4 EASY WALK Results:	5 OFF	6 Intvrl: 17 MILES Results:
Week 17	7 OFF	8 Intvrl: 30 MINUTE RUN Results:	9 EASY WALK Results:	10 Intvrl: 30 MINUTE RUN Results:	11 EASY WALK Results:	12 OFF	13 Intvrl: 5 MILES Results:
Week 18	14 OFF	15 Intvrl: 30 MINUTE RUN Results:	16 EASY WALK Results:	17 Intvrl: 30 MINUTE RUN Results:	18 EASY WALK Results:	19 OFF	20 Intvrl: 6 MILES / MM Results:
Week 19	21 OFF	22 Intvrl: 30 MINUTE RUN Results:	23 EASY WALK Results:	24 Administrative Professionals Day 30 MINUTE RUN Results:	25 EASY WALK Results:	26 OFF	27 Intvrl: 19 MILES Results:
Week 20	28 OFF	29 Intvrl: 30 MINUTE RUN Results:	30 EASY WALK Results:	1 May 2013 30 MINUTE RUN Results:	2 EASY WALK Results:	3 OFF	4 Intvrl: 6 MILES Results:
Week 21	5 OFF	6 Intvrl: 30 MINUTE RUN Results:	7 EASY WALK Results:	8 Intvrl: 30 MINUTE RUN Results:	9 EASY WALK Results:	10 OFF	11 Intvrl: 6 MILES / MM Results:
Week 22	12 Mother's Day OFF	13 Intvrl: 30 MINUTE RUN Results:	14 19th Wedding Anniversary EASY WALK Results:	15 Intvrl: 30 MINUTE RUN Results:	16 EASY WALK Results:	17 OFF	18 Intvrl: 21 MILES Results:
Week 23	19 OFF	20 Intvrl: 30 MINUTE RUN Results:	21 EASY WALK Results:	22 Intvrl: 30 MINUTE RUN Results:	23 EASY WALK Results:	24 OFF	25 Intvrl: 6 MILES Results:
Week 24	26 OFF	27 Memorial Day Intvrl: 30 MINUTE RUN Results:	28 EASY WALK Results:	29 Intvrl: 30 MINUTE RUN Results:	30 EASY WALK Results:	31 OFF	1 June 2013 Goal Weight 215 lbs. 7 MILES Results:
Week 25	2 OFF	3 Intvrl: 30 MINUTE RUN Results:	4 EASY WALK Results:	5 Intvrl: 30 MINUTE RUN Results:	6 EASY WALK Results:	7 OFF	8 Intvrl: 23 MILES Results:
Week 26	9 OFF	10 Intvrl: 30 MINUTE RUN Results:	11 EASY WALK Results:	12 Intvrl: 30 MINUTE RUN Results:	13 EASY WALK Results:	14 Flag Day OFF	15 Intvrl: 7 MILES Results:
Week 27	16 Father's Day OFF	17 Intvrl: 30 MINUTE RUN Results:	18 EASY WALK Results:	19 Intvrl: 30 MINUTE RUN Results:	20 EASY WALK Results:	21 First Day of Summer OFF	22 Intvrl: 6 MILES Results:
Week 28	23 OFF	24 Intvrl: 30 MINUTE RUN Results:	25 EASY WALK Results:	26 OFF	27 7 MILES Results:	28 OFF	29 Intvrl: 30 MINUTE RUN Results:
Week 29	30 OFF	1 July 2013 Intvrl: 30 MINUTE RUN Results:	2 EASY WALK Results:	3 OFF	4 Independence Day 26.2 miles Foot Traffic Flat MARATHON Results:		

Magic Mile (MM)
1. Warm up: 1 slow mile
2. Pace yourself evenly each quarter mile
3. Run as fast as can 1 mile - no puking
4. Walk 5 min. Jog rest of miles for the day

I wrote on this calendar everyday after I had finished my workout and noted my times, distances, intervals, and other notes. This is what my calendar looked like after July 4th:

December 16, 2012 - July 4, 2013

	Sunday	Monday	Tuesday	Wednesday	Thursday	Friday	Saturday
Week 1	16 Dec. 2012 — OFF	17 30/45 sec Intvl: 7.2 miles 30 MINUTE RUN — Results: 41 min.	18 45 min EASY WALK	19 45 min walk 30 MINUTE RUN — Results:	20 45 min walk EASY WALK	21 OFF	22 1/1 min. Intvl: 4 MILES — Results: 4 min.
Week 2	23 OFF	24 1/1 min 30 MINUTE RUN — Results: Knee hurts	25 30 min stat bike EASY WALK	26 45 min stat bike 30 MINUTE RUN — Results: Knee hurts	27 60 min walk EASY WALK — Results: Knee hurts	28 OFF	29 1.5/1 min Intvl: 5 MILES — Results: 5.11 mi.
Week 3	30 OFF	31 60 min stat 30 MINUTE RUN — Results:	1 January 2013 New Year's Day EASY WALK	2 60 min walk 30 MINUTE RUN — Results:	3 60 min walk EASY WALK	4 OFF	5 1.5 min walk Intvl: 2.0 miles — Results:
Week 4	6 OFF	7 MM 10:29 30 MINUTE RUN — Results: 2.5 miles	8 45 min walk EASY WALK	9 stat bike 30 MINUTE RUN — Results:	10 45 min. Pushups EASY WALK cool down	11 OFF	12 60 min Intvl: 2 MILES — Results:
Week 5	13 OFF	14 30 MINUTE RUN — Results: Knee	Shot Triple Cozys EASY WALK — Results: Knee	16 30 MINUTE RUN — Results: Knee	17 pushups EASY WALK cool down — Results: Knee	18 OFF	19 45 min Intvl: 3 MILES — Results: Knee
Week 6	20 OFF	21 45 min walk 30 MINUTE RUN — Results: Stretching	22 60 min walk EASY WALK — Results: Stretching	23 45 min walk 30 MINUTE RUN — Results: Stretch	24 65 min walk EASY WALK	25 OFF	26 body pump 7.5 MILES — Results:
Week 7	27 OFF	28 30 MINUTE RUN — Results:	29 muscles hurt EASY WALK	30 muscles hurt 30 MINUTE RUN — Results:	31 sick EASY WALK	1 February 2013 75 min walk	2 1.5/1 min Intvl: 3 MILES — Results: 3.55
Week 8	3 OFF	4 MM 10:45 30 MINUTE RUN — Results: 2.4 mi.	5 65 min walk EASY WALK	6 4/1 min 30 MINUTE RUN — Results: 3 mi.	7 65 min walk EASY WALK	8 OFF	9 1.5/1 min Intvl: 7 MILES — Results:
Week 9	10 OFF	11 All Running! 30 MINUTE RUN — Results: 2.5 miles	12 OFF EASY WALK	13 46 min walk 30 MINUTE RUN — Results:	14 Valentine's Day 46 min walk EASY WALK	15 OFF	16 1.5/1 min Intvl: 4 MILES — Results:
Week 10	17 OFF	18 run 2 miles 30 MINUTE RUN — Results: 1 mile	19 63 min walk EASY WALK	20 15/1 min 30 MINUTE RUN — Results:	21 OFF	22	23 15/1 min Intvl: 4.80 MILES — Results:
Week 11	24 OFF	25 45 min DVD 30 MINUTE RUN — Results:	26 62 min walk EASY WALK	27 4/1 min 30 MINUTE RUN — Results:	28 OFF	1 March 2013 Goal Weight 240 lbs 235 lbs!!	2 1.5/1 min Intvl: 4 MILES — Results: 8.2 min
Week 12	3 OFF	4 All Run!! 30 MINUTE RUN — Results: 5K!!	5 OFF	6 7 min DVD 30 MINUTE RUN	7 35/1 min EASY WALL	8 OFF	9 5/1 min Intvl: 5 MILES — Results: 2:55
Week 13	10 -100 lbs	11 DVD fully 30 MINUTE RUN — Results:	12 61 min walk EASY WALK	13 2 min walk 30 MINUTE RUN 3 miles	14 OFF EASY WALK	15 64 min walk 3.1 miles	16 2/1 min Intvl: 4 MILES — Results:
Week 14	17 St. Patrick's Day OFF	18 All run 30 MINUTE RUN — Results: 2.5 miles	19 47 min walk EASY WALK	20 64 min walk 30 MINUTE RUN — Results: 3.9 miles	21 OFF EASY WALK	22 OFF	23 2/1 min Intvl: 14 MILES — Results:
Week 15	24 Palm Sunday OFF	25 DVD 30 MINUTE RUN	26 50 min walk EASY WALK	27 2/1 min 40 MINUTE RUN 3.5 miles	28 61 min walk EASY WALK — Results: 2.41 miles	29 Good Friday OFF	30 2/1 min 5 MILES — Results:
Week 16	31 Easter OFF	1 April 2013 2/1 min 30 MINUTE RUN — Results: 3.2 miles	2 54 min walk EASY WALK — Results: 3.2 miles	3 2/1 min 40 MINUTE RUN — Results: 3.6 mi	4 OFF	5	6 2/1 min Intvl: 17 MILES — Results: 3:15
Week 17	7 Soul Lift Fit →	8 stat bike 30 MINUTE RUN — Results:	9 58 min walk EASY WALK	10 63 min walk 30 MINUTE RUN 2.5 miles	11 33 min run a C5K 5K	12 60 min walk OFF 3.2 mi	13 2/1 min 5 MILES — Results:
Week 18	14 OFF	15 All run, 8 min 30 MINUTE RUN 2.5 miles	16 81 min walk EASY WALK — Results: 3.5 miles	17 2/1 min Appa 30 MINUTE RUN — Results: 3.6 mi/8	18 8 min walk EASY WALK 4.8 miles	19 OFF	20 2/1 min 70 6 MILES — Results: 3.12 min
Week 19	21 OFF	22 3/1 min Appa 30 MINUTE RUN — Results: 3 mi	23 64 min walk EASY WALK	24 30 MINUTE RUN — Results: 3.7 mi	25 47 min run slow EASY WALK 6.2 miles	26 OFF	27 2:30/1 min 10 MILES — Results:
Week 20	28 OFF	29 2:30/1 min 30 MINUTE RUN — Results: 2.9 mi	30 52 min walk EASY WALK	1 May 2013 215 lbs 39 min 30 MINUTE RUN 3.25 miles	2 70 min walk EASY WALK 3.9 miles	3 63 min walk OFF 3.5 mi	4 2:30/1 min 6 MILES — Results:
Week 21	5 OFF	6 All run 2 miles 30 MINUTE RUN — Results: 2.6 miles	7 50 min walk EASY WALK — Results: 2.6 miles	8 2:30/1 min 30 MINUTE RUN 3 miles	9 64 min walk 32 min	10 OFF	11 3/1 min 6 MILES — Results: 2:45
Week 22	12 Mother's Day OFF	13 3/1 min 30 MINUTE RUN — Results: 3.1 miles	14 7 min walk EASY WALK 3.5 miles	15 3/1 min 30 MINUTE RUN — Results: 3.4 miles	16 70 min walk EASY WALK	17 OFF	18 3:1 min 21 MILES — Results: 4:39
Week 23	19 OFF	20 mostly run 30 MINUTE RUN — Results: 3.5 miles	21 61 min walk EASY WALK 52 miles	22 stat bike 30 MINUTE RUN 60 min	23 51 min walk EASY WALK 2.75 min	24 43 min walk 2.7 mi OFF	25 3/1 min 6 MILES — Results:
Week 24	26 OFF	27 77 min. 5K 30 MINUTE RUN — Results: 3.2 mi	28 64 min walk 6 miles	29 3/1 min of 60 30 MINUTE RUN 2.35 miles	30 52 min walk EASY WALK 2.75 min	31	1 June 2013 Goal Weight 215 lbs 7/1 MILES 7/1 — Results: 3.2 mi
Week 25	2 OFF	3 run brea 5K 30 MINUTE RUN! 27 min	4 74 min. walk EASY WALK 2.45 miles	5 3/1 min. 30 MINUTE RUN	6 71 min walk EASY WALK	7 OFF	8 1:30/1 min 23 MILES — Results: 1:30
Week 26	9 OFF	10 All run 30 MINUTE RUN 5K	11 54 min walk EASY WALK 2.9 mi	12 2:30/1 min 30 MINUTE RUN 3.5 miles	13 70 min walk EASY WALK 3.9 min	14 Play Day	15 2:30/1 min 6 MILES — Results:
Week 27	16 Father's Day OFF	17 All run 4 mi 30 MINUTE RUN 5K	18 66 min walk EASY WALK 3.75 mi	19 All run 30 MINUTE RUN 5K	20 92 min walk EASY WALK 5.2 mi	21 First Day of Summer OFF	22 2:30/1 min 4 MILES — Results: 70 min
Week 28	23 OFF	24 4/1 min 30 MINUTE RUN 3.2 mi	25 57 min walk — Results: 3.2 mile	26 OFF	27 30/1 min 10 min	28 OFF	29 2:30/1 min 27 MINUTE RUN — Results: 2.5 mi
Week 29	30 OFF	1 July 2013 bonus 40 MINUTE RUN — Results: 4.3 miles	2 OFF EASY WALK	3 2:45/1 min — Results: 11.4 min	4 Independence Day 26.2 Frost Traffic Flat MARATHON 5:06		

Magic Mile (MM)
1. Warm up 1 slow mile
2. Pace yourself every next run/no mile
3. Run as fast as can 1 mile - no pulsing
4. Walk 1 min. jog rest of miles for the day

I had this calendar taped inside the back cover of my journal. I always had it with me. I think it is a great snapshot of my workouts, the plan that I had, and how I kept to it. It helped me to be consistent and not miss a day of exercise. It helped that the little bit of OCD in me wanted to make sure everyday was filled in.

The day before I started this calendar, on December 15th, I ran my first mile without stopping. I ran as fast as I could, (my first magic mile), I did it in 10:40. I remember feeling like I had totally pushed it. I maybe could have run another 100 feet if I was being chased by a tiger, but that was it. I came home that day and was excited to tell my family that I had actually run a mile without stopping; I had never done that before. Even in grade school and middle school I think I stopped and walked when we had to run in P.E.

Other than the first few runs I did, my interval was run 1 minute and then walk 1 minute (1:1). I did this for the first couple weeks, and then I injured my knee. Details on that will be found in my injuries chapter. After my knee got better I ran a (1½:1) interval on my longer Saturday runs, and on my 30 minute midweek runs, I did a (4:1) interval. Then on March 9th I advanced to a (2:1) interval for my longer Saturday runs.

On the day I started my calendar, I finished the book "He Did Deliver Me from Bondage" for the first time. I wrote in my journal on that day:

"Mel and I talked about how being in this choir along with reading this book, changing my life – food, and exercise is really all about coming to Christ and being/ doing the Lords will, and centering my life on Him. This is what I have been reading in this book and overcoming my addictions. I just am very thankful for my Savior and Heavenly Father and prayer; it has been a good week. I just finished the book (for the first time). It has changed my life. Colleen Harrison did a wonderful job opening herself and helping me to do so as well. I am so thankful that Scott gifted me this book and I will continue to learn from it.

I want to write about a lesson last Sunday that Brother Diddy shared in Gospel Doctrine. It was about the Jaredites (Ether). He shared again that the brother of Jared came up with the solution to lighting his ships and went to the Lord in faith to have the Lord make the stones glow after he had already gone to the work of making them. I applied that principle to making enough money to support my family. On Tuesday morning I went to the Lord and presented him that I have been preparing for adding a fourth day at work to support my family and asked him in faith to bless me and my family and he did. It was a wonderful experience, and a principal

I am glad to understand better. Not to just ask for direction, but to come up with a (righteous) solution and then ask and let the Lord bless us."

That evening at my board meeting, they voted to increase my days and thus, my pay. What a great blessing that was.

Another blessing I wish to expand upon is how my MFP friends were very supportive. As I opened up on their forums and got more "pals" I felt accountable to them. They would comment "great day" or "great workout" or "congrats on logging for 100 days." This support was great and important. At one point I posted on the forums about my plans to run a marathon and I got a lot of encouragement. It was fun.

I continued with my workout schedule, my eating routine, and logging on MFP as time went on. Sometime around the 3 month mark I lowered my calories to 1750 a day, as I mentioned before. Thefreedictionary.com says that, "A plan is a program or method worked out beforehand for the accomplishment of an objective and to have a specific aim or purpose." I wrote on December 19th, 2012

"I created and placed a calendar of my workout schedule to the marathon in the back of this book. I like having a plan."

That about sums it up.

CHAPTER 8
Blessings

LET'S START WITH some adventures with the Portland Ensign Choir and Orchestra (PECO). Practice was every Tuesday night in Lake Oswego. I really enjoyed spending the time alone with my wife driving to practice. It gave us a chance to talk about things without the distractions of the house and kids. In fact, singing in the choir together has brought us closer because we are engaged in a good cause. I was also making friends with a couple other tenors and enjoyed their company very much.

In addition to preparing for the PECO Christmas concert, we were also a part of a smaller group of singers in "The Forgotten Carols" conducted by the show's writer, Michael McLean. The performance was on November

23rd, 2012 at the Arlene Schnitzer Concert Hall in downtown Portland. It was an amazing experience. We had to show up early and do a couple dress rehearsals with Michael – it was amazing to be up on stage. I wrote in my journal the day after the performance:

"What a wonderful experience last night, being able to sing in a professional performance. I sat in the choir section in the front row directly behind the piano where Michael played with the spotlight right on him."

Our kids, Mel's mom and my parents were able to attend the performance. There were also a few friends in the audience. It was really a great experience.

The PECO Christmas concert was the next month, just around the corner. There was a Thursday night dress rehearsal, a Friday night performance and then two performances on Saturday - the weekend of December 15th, 2012. It was a tremendous concert. Powerful music and message. Everyone we heard talking about it was raving. I wrote in my journal the following day:

"It was a wonderful experience being in this choir. Oh how I loved singing, using the talent the Lord has given me the best I can. It is awesome. Each concert was about 2 hours long and it was truly

magnificent, everybody that came said they thought it was great and worth the money for tickets. They were $12-18.00 each. Melanie was one of the soloists and the best in my opinion. The whole performance was great; slide shows, a great narration from Ray Summers, and sing-a-longs. Lots of family and friends came, and my mom especially loved it. I saw her crying in the audience and I knew how much she enjoyed seeing me participate in the choir singing, it means so much to her."

The next PECO adventure was singing the National Anthem at a Portland Trailblazers game on January 16th, 2013. How cool is that, to be able to participate at a professional sporting event? In my journal I wrote:

"Mel and I sang with PECO the National Anthem at the Blazer game, it was a really neat experience, to do our sound check with the athletes warming up around us, to be backstage, and then performing under the lights was cool."

The kids came and we stayed after the anthem to watch the game. It was a fun night. Below is a picture of us singing. You can see the side of my head. I'm in the fourth row, just barely left of center, looking off to the side. Melanie is also in there with her face hidden.

The last PECO adventure was that I had to keep exchanging my tuxedo for smaller ones. The lady that was over the uniforms (dresses and tuxedos) was pretty surprised by the changes in my size that were happening. Thank goodness they allowed me to keep getting ones that fit correctly.

Another significant event that happened was when I received a priesthood blessing. From the very beginning of my journey I had wanted a priesthood blessing but didn't feel like the time was right until Sunday, February 10th, 2013. I knew a priesthood blessing in this situation could provide words of comfort, guidance, and direction, if given by a worthy holder of the Melchizedek Priesthood. The Melchizedek Priesthood allows you to act under the direction of Heavenly Father and Jesus Christ. This is done by the laying on of hands. It is sacred and personal. I share this experience with you because it was important in my journey.

At church on Sunday the 10th I asked Scott and Ty if they would come over and give me a blessing and they agreed to come that evening. I remember feeling like it didn't matter who or which one of them gave me the blessing, I just wanted whoever it was to feel like they were the right person. That evening when they came over, Scott asked if he could give the blessing. Both Scott and Ty had discussed it on the way over and decided Scott should do it.

The blessing was tremendous. It was the first time in my life I wrote down in my journal the things said in one of my blessings. I wanted to remember it. I have, on many occasions throughout this journey, gone back and reread that journal entry. Here are some of the words from my blessing;

- That the Lord loves me.
- I should study my patriarchal blessing.
- To council with my wife.

- He said that the Lord is happy with the changes I've made.

- They will extend my life.

- I will be there for my kids and grandkids.

- He spoke of my property in Cathlamet where I have had many serious issues and trials in the past 6 years. He told me that those issues would be resolved and the people helping me with that situation would have the spirit aiding *them*. (Several months later on July 22nd, 2013 I sold the property and the title was recorded in the new owners' name. This was a truly amazing blessing my family's life and one I feared may never happen.)

- He referred to my employment and said it would change and I would be blessed in my new career. This was a shocker!! I thought things were going really well at work; I was happy and had even started working another day each week as I previously mentioned.

The next few months I tried to ignore that he had said anything about my job. I was perplexed and distraught even thinking about it. I started getting the feeling in April or May that there was going to be a career change. Then, on June 14th, 2013 my employment ended and I knew, even believed that better things were in store and a new direction was soon to come. It was difficult being unemployed again, but surprisingly, it was beneficial to me, my family, and church service. I knew it was a fulfillment of the words in that blessing. I knew greater things were to come. Because I was unemployed during that next summer, I was able to do many things that were good for the young men and the activities we had planned. It also gave me a couple of weeks to prepare for my marathon without the stress of having to work.

CHAPTER 9
Weigh-in #2

WEIGH-IN #2 WAS approaching and things were roll along. Official weigh-in #2 was scheduled for March 1st, 2013. My goal was to weigh 240 lbs. I wasn't nervous for this weigh-in because I knew I was going to make it. I had been weighing less than 240 lbs for a week or so now. Scott and Ty came over at 6am for the big moment. Here is the link for the video of the weigh-in and the QR code for scanning: http://bit.ly/powerwithin3

I weighed in at 235.8 lbs. I had lost 96.6 lbs. in the first 6 months! I had surpassed my goal by more than 4 lbs! Those are some big numbers. My plan was working. I was doing it! It was a great feeling.

I was so glad both Scott and Ty were there this time for the weigh-in. My friendships are strong with each of them, but each friendship is different. They are some of my bestfriends, and I am immensely grateful for them. I can't say that enough. They are amazing men. It feels like a complete team when we are all together.

That evening was my reward. It was awesome! Scott, Ty and I all went on a triple date with our wives and we had an incredible time. We started by going to Thai Orchid in downtown Vancouver, WA for a great sushi and Thai dinner. The conversation was relaxed and we all got along great. There was lots of laughter. After dinner we went into Portland and had amazing desserts at Pix Patisserie! It was a perfect reward, being together and having fun. It was a reward for all of us. I think that Scott, Ty, and I all felt like it was well deserved for our wives as well since they always supported us and spent time away from us as we were working out and training. Here is a picture of the evening. It was taken by Ty so he's not in the picture. This was right after we got our desserts and were so excited that our eyes seemed to be glowing.

9 days later I finally lost 100 lbs. 100 lbs. lost!! For anybody on a weight loss journey this is a momentous occasion. That's a lot of weight! I had decided about a month earlier that when I hit this mark I was going to

reward myself with a new cell phone, but not any phone - a "smartphone." It had been 5 or 6 years since my last phone upgrade and I was way past due. My current phone was barely "textable."

I had done some research and really wanted the Samsung Galaxy Note II, but they were so expensive. $299 with an upgrade and a new 2 year contract. So in the days before I reached the 100 lb mark I started researching online and saw that my carrier had the refurbished Galaxy S3 for only $29.99! I decided to get the refurbished phone since it was a great phone and a great deal. The next day, I weighed myself and I was 0.2 lbs away from losing 100 lbs. I decided I didn't want a reward for something I hadn't actually done, so I would wait another day. I checked the website and the phones were still available. The next morning I weighed myself again, AND I WAS STILL 0.2 lbs. away. I think I weighed myself 3 times that morning to see if it would change, but it didn't. A little frustrated I decided not to get the reward that day because the stupid scale still said "NO."

The next day, March 10th, 2013 I got on the scale and I had done it! 100 lbs lost! I immediately went to the computer and checked for phones. My carrier was having a one day only sale on a refurbished Samsung Galaxy Note

II for only $.99. Yes, 99 cents! I couldn't believe it, I was super excited! It was a huge blessing and another miracle in my journey. I bought one for myself and for Melanie since she was eligible for an upgrade as well. How cool is that?! Because I waited until I had actually reached 100 lbs. lost, I was able to get the phone I really wanted for an incredible deal.

This phone has been a huge blessing in my life and another key component to my success. It wasn't critical, but it has simplified my journey with the mobile version of MyFitnessPal, other fitness apps, and access to GPS. The greatest blessing I have received through this (phone-tablet) phablet smartphone has been the spiritual benefits of having the LDS Gospel Library. There are so many talks by General Authorities and available access to items of a spiritual nature.

The Lord had poured out his spirit upon me and I was changed – inside and out. My life was different. I wasn't who I had always identified myself to be. Change was affecting all of me. I still had, and have, so far to go. I felt like I was in the wash cycle of a washing machine – getting the old dirty past out, but still needing a good rinse and drying. My journey continues...

CHAPTER 10

Injuries

THE PLAN FROM the very beginning was to complete this journey injury free, a goal that was accomplished. There was plenty of pain and some close calls but nothing major. The first aches and pains I felt were shin splints. They started when I began walking, but I didn't let them keep me from exercising. I continued walking through the pain and after a couple of weeks they stopped. There were ankle twinges and aching feet, the bottoms of my feet were especially sore in the beginning. I don't think there was ever a time when I worked out when something didn't hurt or was sore. At night I slept with my feet out of the covers because they felt better in the cool air.

In mid to late December 2012, I was at the movies

with Beyden when my left knee started hurting right below the knee cap. At that time I didn't know what caused it and was thoroughly confused and pretty upset. I continued my workouts as scheduled for the next week and a half making note on my calendar, that my "knee hurts" along with the other data. At Scott's suggestion, I started a series of ibuprofen for 2 weeks taking 600mg a day and icing my knee every night. Icing is not fun. It hurts. I was hoping that over time I would get used to icing, but I haven't. It's still unpleasant. It's still cold, and it still hurts. I would ice my knee for about 20 minutes at a time. At the same time I started taking ibuprofen I started taking a triple omega supplement at Mike's suggestion. I'm not sure it has helped, but I know it hasn't hurt or been bad, so I have continued to take one everyday. I think it is good for my heart and my joints.

On January 9th, 2013 I stopped walking and running and began core work including sit-ups and pushups to help my knee recover. My January 12th, 2013 journal entry reads:

"Scott has me not running or using the stationary bike for the last couple days and for the next week at least. This has been very hard and demoralizing for me. This is because my left knee has been

hurting for 3 weeks now and we feel that it is from being a little to aggressive with the workouts and I have to lay off it so it can heal and not become a bigger injury. He wants me to do pushups and sit-ups and things."

On January 21st, 2013 I started a stretching routine. I had not done any stretching before this point and Scott told me I needed to. For some reason, I was resistant to the idea. I think it is partially because of the extra time it takes, and I was uneducated about how to stretch and why it would help. Scott told me what stretches to do and I did some research on the internet and came up with 4 stretches I would do before and after every run. I made a sheet to teach me how to do the stretches and I put it in my journal. Here is the sheet:

ILIOTIBIAL
BAND STRETCHES

HAMSTRING STRETCH

Quad
stretch

Butterfly
stretch

Calf Stretch

I would start with the iliotibial (IT) band stretch, and I found an IT band stretch in a video on YouTube that really worked fantastic. It showed me that I should stand at a counter or table that was about waist high, about 6-10 inches from the edge and lay my foot on the counter with the outer ankle down and knee pointing out to the side. I would then bend at my waist to stretch the IT band. I think this stretch had a significant impact on my knee injury healing. I would then stretch my hamstrings, quads, and finally calves. I would hold each stretch for about 10 seconds on each leg before every workout and 30 seconds on each leg after the workout was complete.

The same day I started my stretching routine, I also started walking again. I wrote in my journal on January 24th, 2013:

"I started walking again this week. Today is Thursday and I have walked the last 4 days. I have stretched before and after each time and I think it is helping. I stopped taking the ibuprofen today and my knee is a little tender. I am not going to run/walk tomorrow, I want a rest day. It really has done a lot for my mental state to get out and get the heart rate up. I'm nervous to run because I don't want it to hurt again."

On February 2nd, 2013 I started my interval running again. I began wearing a neoprene knee brace on my injured knee every time I ran. I borrowed it from my brother-in-law. I wore this brace up to and during the marathon and I really think it helped. However, it gave me terrible acne on my thigh and knee which I hated.

My least favorite injury recurred many times. Bloody nipples. Painful. The first time I got them was after my 17.85 mile run. I was at the coast in Seaside, Oregon on April 6th, 2013. I was running in a serious coastal storm with rain flying *up* in my face the whole time. When I got back from the run I was so exhausted that I didn't even notice the injury until I stood in the shower. HOLY CRAP that was a shocker and hurt like the dickens! They eventually healed, only to be injured again. I learned that if I put antiperspirant on them before my shorter runs it helped. I soon found that I could cover them with athletic tape before my long runs to avoid pain and injury. I hoped in the beginning that I would eventually get tougher nipples and they would become resistant to injury – let's just say that they never did, and it was a hard lesson learned.

One of the major things I did to help with recovery was ice baths. After hard workouts I would fill my tub with cold water, as cold as I could get it, add ice and then sit in the tub for 15-25 minutes. I did this after every workout where I felt like I had really exhausted my leg muscles.

Most often just my Saturday runs. I believe it made a huge difference and helped my leg recovery go from 3 to 4 days, to only 1 day. It wasn't fun, but I passed the time in the tub writing in my journal, texting my workout updates, and focusing on the knowledge that it was going to help my recovery in the "long run." I still do this after my hard workouts. Here is a picture:

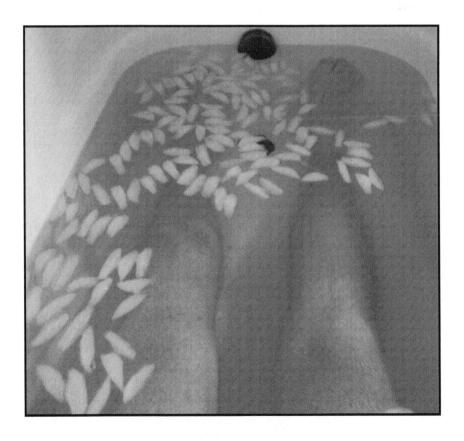

Another thing I do to help with injury prevention is rhythmic breathing. I read about this in an online article from Runner's World titled "Running on Air: Breathing Techniques" by Budd Coates and Claire Kowalchik. Rhythmic breathing is a method of breathing while running that helps prevent injury and increases performance. A simple explanation is that you want to breathe out while running on alternating sides of your body. This means you are not always exhaling when you plant your left foot down or vice versa. The theory behind it, as I understand, is that when you breathe out your body is in a more relaxed state and more prone to injury. If you are always exhaling on the same side then you will be at risk of increased injury on that side. The breathing method took a while to get used to, but I was able to get it with some concentration and practice. It's all about alternating the sides you exhale on. I now can run and not have to think too hard to implement this technique. It comes more naturally now. I have also noticed that I run faster and with better posture while using this breathing method.

The basic technique is to breath in (inhale) for a counted number of even or odd steps, and then to breath out (exhale) on the opposite even or odd. So, for example, if you are running at a relaxed pace, then breathe in for 4 steps and breathe out for 3 steps, or 4-3. This will insure that you will rotate your exhales on the left and right sides.

If you are running at faster more vigorous pace then do a 3-2 rhythmic breathing series. For the times you are running uphill or really pushing it, you can do a 2-1 breathing series, and if you are really really pushing it you can do a 2-1-1-1 breathing series.

When I was talking to Scott about my level of pain tolerance, I told him it was 5 out of 10. Today I think that has improved to a 6. It is important to note that the lessons learned from pain, discomfort, and injuries have been very valuable and made me a better athlete.

CHAPTER 11

The Long Runs – "Exercising" Faith

PHYSICAL EXERCISE IS painful – sometimes very painful, but the more you do it the faster and stronger you will become. Exercising faith is exactly the same, it is painful and difficult but will make you stronger, happier, and eventually become easier. In this chapter I am going to chronicle the longer runs that I did in preparation for the marathon. More importantly, I am going to share the fact that it was within these long runs that many things changed, not just in my body, but in my spirit and soul.

A major part of training for a marathon is the long run. They are foreboding, nerve racking, and painful, but very necessary. As you saw from my calendar, I planned my long runs for Saturdays. I always got an early start, and that was for a few reasons. First, the marathon I signed up for started at 6am and I wanted to become accustomed to running this early in the morning. For instance, I trained my body to go to the bathroom early so I would go *before* my long run. I wanted to figure out what and how much I should eat before my long runs to see what my body liked best. It is also usually cooler in the morning which I like better for running. After each long run, it would take me a couple hours to cool down, stretch, eat, take my ice bath, shower, and get dressed so that I was to the point where I could hobble around for a while. By starting earlier I was also able to finish earlier and do other things later that day with my family and friends. I am going to list each run with some detail and then post them again in a table so you can see the progression.

My first long run was on February 9th, 2013. I ran 7.5 miles with a run walk interval of (1½:1) minute, meaning I would run for 90 seconds and then walk for 60 seconds. This run took me 93 minutes. I did this run starting at my house and running through the neighborhood and looping around a nearby Costco and then back to my place. I didn't write anything about it in my journal so it must have been a good run.

The second long run was on February 23rd, 2013. I ran 9.5 miles with an interval of (1½:1) minute. This run took me 118 minutes, so almost 2 hours. I ran from my house, through the neighborhood, to the end of Klineline Park or Salmon Creek trail, and back. This trail is one of my favorite places to run or ride my bike. I enjoy it very much and have done it with family and friends many times. It was on this trail that I ran and rode my bike for the very first time during my journey.

The third long run was on March 9th, 2013. I ran 13.1 miles – a half marathon with an interval of (2:1) minute. This run took me 2 hours and 33 minutes. This run was originally planned as a 12 mile run, but the day before, Scott called me and told me that the Clark County Runners Club was having a half marathon and that I was doing it with him. The race was in Washougal, WA. We ran the race there on the dike. I started the race a half hour early so I would finish not too far behind everyone else. Scott and I ran our own races, and it was great to have him there. It was an exciting accomplishment – my first half marathon!

The fourth long run was on March 23rd, 2013. I ran 14 miles with an interval of (2:1) minute. This run took me 2 hours and 50 minutes. This run was an out and back from my home, through the Burnt Bridge Creek Trail to the 7 mile mark, and then back home. After that run I wrote in my journal, while I was in the ice bath, stating that I had simply completed it.

The fifth long run was on April 6th, 2013. I ran 17.85 miles with an interval of (2:1) minute. This run took me 3 hours and 45 minutes. This is the run I did at the coast in Seaside, Oregon and was a very difficult run. I ran over half of it on the beach which I thought would be good, giving a little extra cushion because of the sand, but that actually ended up being a detriment. Since I had done all of my walking and running to this point pounding pavement, running on the softer surface wreaked havoc on my feet. This run was very stormy and the wind was terrible. Running with the wind was great! It gave a sense of weightlessness. Running soaking wet however, was miserable. The heavy, wet clothes, sweat, the road spray from the cars driving by (I ran 6 miles on highway 101), and the bloody nipples I mentioned before all added to the misery. The last 2 miles were tough. I didn't think I was going to make it, but I didn't stop. I just needed to get it done. One of the most important things to do in preparing for a marathon is increase your distances.

The sixth long run was on April 27th, 2013. I ran 19 miles with an interval of (2½:1) minute. This run took me

3 hours and 49 minutes. This run was a big loop from my house down Klineline and then up around the Clark County fairgrounds and back home. This was a great run, I felt good. I actually completed it in the same time as my last long run but went more than a mile further. This run was very spiritual and an emotional one for me. There were times I was weeping while I was running but not from pain, it was from overwhelming spiritual realizations. I will share more of this later.

The seventh long run was on May 18th, 2013. I ran 21.5 miles with an interval of (3:1) minute. This run took me 4 hours and 39 minutes. This run was also a big loop from my house out the opposite direction from the last. I went down 72nd to 199th to 142nd then down 119th to home. This run was hard. It was even worse than the beach run. I don't like to dwell on the misery. I remember around mile 10 my legs started to hurt and I had to go to the bathroom and there was nowhere to go until mile 19. Those were 9 miserable miles. It was also on roads that were not good for running; they had no shoulders, and heavy traffic. Looking back though, this run was important for a couple reasons; I completed it, it was a mental victory, and now I had a bad run to which I could compare to my good ones.

The eighth and last long run before the marathon was

on June 8th, 2013. I ran 23 miles with an interval of (2½:1) minute. This run took me 4 hours and 30 minutes. This run was the bridges loop. I started at my brother's house and ran around the I5 Bridge to the I205 Bridge and back to my brother's house. This was an amazing run and I will also share more of this run later in this chapter.

Here are all the above runs at a glance to see the progression:

Date	Miles	Interval	Time
2-9-13	7.5 miles	1½:1	1 hour 33 minutes
2-23-13	9.5 miles	1½:1	1 hour 58 minutes
3-9-13	13.1 miles	2:1	2 hour 33 minutes
3-23-13	14 miles	2:1	2 hour 50 minutes
4-6-13	17.85 miles	2:1	3 hour 45 minutes
4-27-13	19 miles	2½:1	3 hour 49 minutes
5-18-13	21.5 miles	3:1	4 hour 39 minutes
6-8-13	23 miles	2½:1	4 hour 30 minutes

Achieving these runs helped prepare me to complete the marathon. I could not have done it without them. They prepared me physically, mentally, and emotionally.

More importantly, I learned spiritual things on my long runs. I learned things about the Spirit, the Gospel of Jesus Christ, and what the Lord requires of me - things that I wouldn't have learned otherwise. These lessons seemed to come often as I was in the middle of one of these runs, physically pushing my body to its limits. Those thoughts, those lessons, those miracles are something that have changed my life even more than losing 140 lbs. This is what is making me a better father, husband, brother, son, and servant. Here are some of the spiritual lessons I learned. They are very dear to me.

One of the aha moments came before I started any of my long runs. It was a learning moment as I sought for the Spirit. Sunday morning November 4th, 2012, I wrote in my journal:

"I have been reading the book "He Did Deliver Me from Bondage" and I was struck by the nature of agency and its eternality – continuousness. I guess I had thought as the author had previously thought that heaven was a place of complete joy / freedom where we couldn't sin or separate ourselves from God. Where in fact, agency is very much present in Heaven, only that God is perfect and would not choose to sin – ever, and if this eternal principal didn't exist there would be no God or Heaven. I don't think I ever thought of it like that. I just read my patriarchal blessing; it was very powerful for me to read. I definitively felt the Spirit, and very strongly in certain places as I read it. I am thankful that I have the Spirit again and I want it to be with me always. It all comes down to choice and

obedience. I don't know if it becomes easier, but I do believe it can become a habit. Perfection isn't a place; it is a state of CHOICE. Being perfect is a state of CHOICE. Free agency is important and eternal. We all go through trials to learn how important agency is. In the book it said willpower is our will and His (God's) power = Will-Power."

The next spiritual insight I received was the spiritual connection between the body and the spirit. Before I started this journey I never would have believed the connection between a healthy physical body and a strong spirit. The concept occurred to me at a varsity scout prep hike for our backpacking trip we did the summer of 2013. On this "hike" we went on a 4 mile loop with our backpacks from the church on side streets. During the hike I was talking to Roy Pyatt, a good friend of mine and an advisor for the boys. Roy is an amazing scriptorian and a great guy who is full of the Spirit. As I hiked with Roy, we had a great conversation about where I was in my journey and what was happening in my life. At one point he mentioned that there is a scripture that talks about the renewing of bodies and its connection to the Spirit. When he said this a bell went off in my head and I was touched by the Spirit. It made so much sense to me, and I wanted to ponder this concept for a while. Later I found the scripture in Doctrine and Covenants section 84, verse 30 that says, "...sanctified by the Spirit unto the renewing of their bodies."

Later another friend shared with me a passage in Mormon Doctrine on pg. 276 under the subject of Compliance with the law of the fast. It said that President Joseph F. Smith said fasting, "...would call attention to the sin of overeating, place the body in subjection to the spirit, and so promote communion with the Holy Ghost, and insure a spiritual strength and power which the people of the nation so greatly need." As I pondered and lived the Law of the fast, my body was getting healthier, and I saw changes happening in my own life.

These changes in my life brought up the following thoughts. When have I ever seen a morbidly obese Apostle? – Never. The first time I thought that it hit me like a ton of bricks. Sure a couple have a few extra pounds, but none are morbidly obese, from my observation. This is not a coincidence.

The body is an instrument in how the spirit reacts or manifests itself physically. When one feels the spirit, it is felt physically, and can be felt in many different ways and is different for each individual. The feelings of joy, peace, and love can be felt by goose bumps, tingling, burning in the bosom, warm sensation, comfort, patience, inspiration, and many, many other good feelings. When the body is healthy I have found that the Spirit responds differently and in turn is sanctifying and purifying in a spiritual way. Having had both a fat, unhealthy body and a healthy body, I have felt the difference. I know that a healthy body will only ENHANCE a healthy spirit. As I have shared this connection between the body and spirit with family and friends it has strengthened my knowledge that this principle is true. It has been confirmed to me many times. I have often felt the skepticism or doubt from someone as I talk about this and I understand that. I don't think that when I was fat I would have believed it if someone had told me this either. But that is the point, don't take my word for it – find out for yourself.

The next insight I had was again connected to the eternal principal of free agency. This principle is DEEPLY engrained in me and my patriarchal blessing even refers to this personal trait in me. I have always been obedient, but I would usually put my own twist or edge on things. This is how I expressed my agency at times – "it was my choice" would ring in my head. There have been situations when I would make a good choice, but then tweak it just a little bit so that it was a little irreverent, or more humorous. This became an expression of my personality and part of how I identified myself. Through this journey I have come to realize and understand that free agency is something different. This was a difficult realization and even harder to put into action. I had an experience on my 19 mile run on April 27th, 2013, which I described in my journal entry the following day:

"Yesterday I was up early and out for my 19 mile run. I left about 6:15am. As I ran I listened to the latest conference talks. I got through much of it as I ran for over 3 hours and 45 minutes. At one point around mile 9 I had a spiritual moment when my spirit was being renewed and it really sunk in that my deeply engrained right to choose (free agency) isn't about choosing what I want, but what the Lord wants. Christ's words "not my will, but thine, be done." (Luke 22:42) really reverberated with me and I wept uncontrollably. Those that saw me running and weeping must have thought that I was in a lot of pain, not knowing I was overcome by the Spirit."

One of the hardest but most wonderful lessons for me to learn was that I have free agency given to me by God – not so I can do what I want, but so I can freely choose to give my agency back to Him and do HIS will. This is one gem of knowledge I hope anyone who reads this book remembers and lives. I believe this to be part of what enduring to the end means. This is one of the most powerful lessons learned in my life and is a daily battle to remember it and live it; I testify that life is so much better when lived this way. My patriarchal blessing says "to always seek his counsel first in all things." It is a principal I have read many times and counsel that I love.

Associated with this principle of free agency in my mind is the scriptural admonition to "pray always" (Luke 21:36). This was how I started to seek his counsel in all things – through prayer. In my journal entry on May 2nd, 2013 I wrote:

"The last few days I must have said "my dear Heavenly Father" 300 times. I always thought continual prayer meant a prayer in your heart. I'm learning that for me it's saying a prayer every time I do something to get His direction. I have honestly strived this week to do the Lords will and put him first – seek him first and the Spirit has been with me more often. I want to continue to be guided. That is why I am writing in my journal now. It is what I felt I should do after one of my prayers."

Next down this spiritual journey was learning the difference between when I have the spirit with me and when I don't. One of the clearest examples of this in my life was the difference felt between my 21.5 mile run and my 23 mile run. The 21 mile run was hard, the pain started early and got worse and I wasn't feeling the Spirit. It helped me to understand that running with the Spirit is easier than running without it. My 23 mile run was longer but took less time, and it was full of the Spirit. Let me share more.

A few days before my 23 mile run I was having severe anxiety and needed comfort. I called my wife and she suggested I ask Scott for another priesthood blessing. I want to share again some of the things from that blessing, with particular attention to the circle of influence for good I referenced earlier. Journal entry from June 4th, 2013:

"He said my circle of influence will be great and that is one of the things the Lord is concerned with. Those that I can influence/help for good, for his purposes. He blessed me with comfort and to have patience. He said that the Lord will bless me. He mentioned there will be hard work. He said my anxiety would go away. These blessings come through obedience. He said I need meekness. I looked that up to get a better definition and it says quiet, gentle, patient, longsuffering, and submissive."

In talking with Scott that day he shared with me how receiving direction, revelation, or inspiration can be like being in a fog; when you look out you are only able to see far enough ahead to go in the right direction, but not see the destination. You can't always see the end of the path, lesson, or trial, but you see enough to keep moving forward.

My June 8th, 2013 journal entry:

"I'm back from my 23 mile run today and I have so much I need to write. I'm sitting in an ice bath again writing and texting. I parked at Lance's (my brother) house and started from there. I did the bridges loop running down across the I-5 Bridge and then back down Marine Drive and back across I-205 Bridge. Some significant things happened while I was running. As a note I listened to Neal A. Maxwell talks the whole time. What an awesome Apostle he was."

I witnessed miracles on this run. They are very personal to me, as are a lot of my experiences; however I feel that it is important that I share them.

The first one was at mile 10. I remember when it happened because I purposefully took out my phone and checked what mile I was on by using my GPS. It was there that I received confirmation that the Lord wanted me to write *this* book so that I may help others to <u>know</u> Christ, to share my journey as a witness; that Christ is real and the Savior of all mankind. Sharing my witness is one way I can best serve my Father's children and have a circle of influence that is good. Mile 10 is when I knew I wanted to title the book, "The Power Within" because Christ is the power in each of us and His message is one of happiness, peace, work, and love. He wants the best for us and wants us to live eternally in His presence. This was another weeping/running moment for me.

The second miracle that happened on this run involves my brother. As I stated in the very beginning of this book, my brother and I were the youngest kids in our family, following 5 older sisters. He is 2 years older than me and while I was the fat, funny kid, he was the popular jock competing in high school and college athletics. All my life I have wanted to connect with my *only* brother, but we've had continual struggles and it has never worked out. We talked, but didn't truly communicate with each other. I want my brother and his family to know how much I love and admire them. As I write, I cry because of the love I feel for them.

He knew I was running the bridges loop because I had asked him about the route, and had parked my car at his house. At mile 20, out of nowhere I got a text from my brother asking me where I was. I texted him back and gave him an answer. I was actually running down the middle of Marine Drive along the yellow line because the Blue Lake Triathlon was going that day and the road was closed to car traffic. The shoulders of the road were packed with the racers riding their road bikes during the bike leg. At one point, one of the police officers on his motorcycle came along side of me and said it was a good choice to run down the middle of the road because there was nowhere else to safely do it. A few minutes later my brother showed up on his road bike and met me just before I ran across the I-205 Bridge. He brought me "fuel" (energy bar and electrolyte tablets) and water and said I was doing a good job and had a quick conversation as I continued on my run. This was HUGE. I think it was the start of better things to come for me and my brother. He came at exactly the point in the run when I needed help the most. I know that prayers were answered that day with his actions and his willingness to be there for me.

By this point, we know that exercise is hard and it hurts, but that it's worth it because of the additional strength you gain both physically and spiritually. I would admonish you to council with the Lord in all thy doings, seeking the will of the Lord with each decision you make; which is principle 11 from the book – "He Did Deliver Me from Bondage." It asks this question; and I quote from page 149-150. "How do you do that? You take the first three steps every morning of your life. (1) I'm powerless to know the right things to do this day, but (2) God knows exactly what the right thing is for me and for everyone, so (3) I'll turn my will and life over to Him and trust Him in all things this day – including His power to direct my life. I will trust His voice to me. I will pray – not for this thing or that thing, for I do not know if this or that is the best policy. I will pray only for a knowledge of His will for me and the power to carry that out."

CHAPTER 12
Weigh-in #3

MY THIRD OFFICIAL weigh-in was on June 1st, 2013. It was the 9 month mark and Scott and Ty came over at 5:20 in the morning. My goal weight for this weigh-in was 215 lbs. Here is the link and QR code to watch that weigh-in video: http://bit.ly/powerwithin4

I weighed-in at 203.4 lbs. I had lost a total of 129 lbs. so far! I had already reached the 215 lb. goal a month earlier, in May, so there wasn't any nervousness about hitting this goal. I was well into my marathon training and only a month away from the race now. I felt great and there was a definite physical change in my body.

In the video Scott asks me "how I feel" and I reply "cold". This wasn't a quip or me trying to be funny. I was cold because I had very little clothes on and a lot less fat! I finally understood the chronic coldness my wife suffered from her entire life. I am cold all the time now. This is something that I have never really experienced before and I don't particularly like it. My body has much less insulation than it used to and I think that bodies take time to calibrate after such a dramatic change. Before losing weight I was always hot and tended to wear as little clothing as possible. I have a running joke with more than one of my friends about being pantless. Before I lost weight, the first thing I did when I got home was remove my pants. They would cut into my waist and it was uncomfortable. I was also hot and I felt relief having them off. I think people, especially men, everywhere know what I'm talking about. When friends showed up at my house they knew that it would take me a few minutes to answer the door because I usually had to go to my room and put on pants. Good friends and family knew that they would just have to see me with them off! It was one of my quirks. I liked the conversation it started and shock factor it possessed.

The reward for achieving this weigh-in goal didn't actually occur for over a month. It happened one day after the marathon on July 5th, 2013. Scott, Ty, and I went golfing. It was fantastic. It was the first time I had been golfing in 15 years. I hadn't even swung a club up until then. It was a funny sight I'm sure, since we all kind of hobbled along, carrying our clubs for 9 holes, sore and stiff from the race the day before. It was a beautiful day, but the conversation was one that I didn't understand. Scott and Ty talked about road race bike stuff and I was clueless as to what they meant by any of it. Other than that, it was actually a great way to get out and use and stretch our leg muscles to help in recovering from the race. Towards the end of the round I actually started hitting some good shots! Scott and Ty did great the whole time. That experience made me think that I would love to continue to golf as time and money permit. It was lots of fun and it was great to be with them.

This third weigh-in brought to light many pros and

cons to my new weight loss. Around this time in my journey I diagnosed myself with postural hypotension or low blood pressure. This affects me when I stand up. I get very light headed and dizzy – I haven't fainted yet but have steadied myself on a table, wall, or chair, many times. I have hoped that this would improve over the months and my body would adjust itself, but alas, it still happens daily. That is a just another challenge I have experienced in my journey.

On the contrary, one of the benefits so far is that I have stopped using my continuous positive airway pressure (CPAP) machine for my sleep apnea. All of my sleep apnea symptoms have been absent for months now. Mel says I no longer snore or stop breathing in my sleep. I am thrilled I am healthier. This was actually one of the initial reasons I wanted to lose weight. I know many will hear this and think I am crazy, but after taking 3 months of fighting to tolerate the machine, I then started to really like it and looked forward to using it every night. It became very comforting to me. I miss it to this day and my wife keeps bugging me to take the machine off of my end table and pack it up, but I still have it sitting there like an old friend.

I also hope I have reduced my risk for diabetes. I have

never been diagnosed as pre-diabetic – but it runs on both sides of my family and I believed I would have gotten it if I hadn't changed. My maternal grandmother had it and my father has it. Let's hope that this trial will not manifest itself and it will pass over me.

Cutting my toenails is much easier now since I'm not trying to bend over the weight of another person to reach them. It used to be a serious workout for me when I cut my toenails. Now I just "get-r-done" – it's great! I've asked Mel our entire marriage if she would cut my toenails, but she has always gracefully declined.

One task that is a little more challenging is getting the lint out of my belly button. It seems as though my sagging skin has collapsed into a cavernous space once known as my belly button. As a result, the retrieval of the lint isn't what it used to be – who knew?

On June 15th, 2013 I weighed-in at less than 200 lbs. This was a huge mark to hit – being in "one-derland" (pr. wonderland) was awesome. This is a weight I hadn't seen since I was in middle school, and didn't think I would ever see again. I had talked to family and friends of hitting this mark many times. I took a picture of the scale that morning as actual proof and texted it to some loved ones.

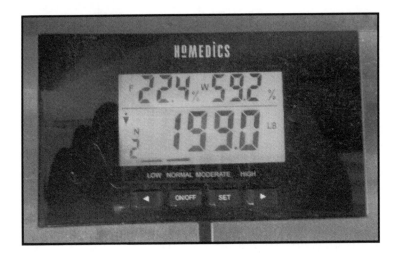

One of the unexpected things I now love is seeing walkers, runners, and people exercising while I'm driving around. I used to drive around and notice things like food places, (especially my favorite places to eat) and cool cars. Now I **LOVE** seeing people running, getting their exercise on, and training for their next race. ESPECIALLY FAT PEOPLE! On August 29th, 2012 I wrote in my journal something I think most fat people think.

"When I went for a walk this morning I was pretty bothered to be the fat guy working out, it's just the way that people look at fat people when they exercise, and the things they sometimes think."

I couldn't have been more wrong! I'm so glad I didn't let that stop me (like I had in the past) from exercising. As

I'm driving down the road or doing my own workout for the day THERE IS NOTHING I LIKE MORE THAN SEEING FAT PEOPLE EXERCISING! They're out there working out and I love it. I KNOW how hard it is, and how it hurts. Don't ever let thoughts like the ones I had stop you; you are inspiring more people than you could ever comprehend, including me. I also appreciate the roads and sidewalks that are running and cycling friendly, so much more now. That's something I had never considered before and now I see how important it is.

This brings me to my most recent, biggest, pet peeve. I hate wearing clothes that are too big for me. I'm not sure exactly why, but I hate it. Its probably vanity, but it takes me back (mentally) to the old, fat guy. It makes me think that I'm still that fat guy and I still have all that fat guy emotional and mental "baggage". On the contrary, when I wear clothes that fit properly I feel good – great – confident – like the new me, the person I'm becoming, that frankly everyone likes better, especially myself. So needless to say, I DO NOT LIKE BAGGY CLOTHES. I'm glad that thrift stores exist.

So, through the course of this journey I have been to Goodwill a dozen times getting clothes that fit; a shirt, pants, or workout clothes as I could afford it. I always picked clothes that had the ½ off weekly color tag – they were such a great deal. I could get a shirt for $2-3.00, or pants for $4.00. It's also been great to have 10 times the choices than I used to as a fat guy. I'm even able to borrow clothes from my *15 year old son* on occasion. That has been really weird for both of us. It is also really cool that wearing his clothes is not a joke now like it used to be. More than a few times I have reenacted the Chris Farley scene of "Fat Guy in a Little Coat" from the movie Tommy Boy for family and friends, and have always gotten a good laugh. Now the coat fits!

The day before my third weigh-in I shaved my beard. I wanted to see what I looked like without a beard. The last time I shaved it was probably 13 years ago when the kids were little, and I let it grow right back. So for the majority of my adult life I had a full beard. I started wearing it mainly because I wanted to hide my 3 chins and it gave some definition to my face. Also, I had a bit of a baby face without it. I liked my beard. After I shaved, I was surprised to see how much I looked like my brother and how much some of my nephews looked like me.

A few days after shaving one of my nephews was having his wedding reception, and many of my siblings were there. I went to the reception in clothes that fit. One of my sisters didn't even recognize me; she had walked right by me 3 times and didn't realize who I was. Then a few minutes later she was standing, back to me, in front of me talking to Mel and asked her where I was. Mel slowly turned her around; she looked at me and was so surprised. I think she exclaimed "Oh!" She turned red with embarrassment at the fact that she hadn't recognized me. We talked for awhile about how different I was and how good I looked.

A week or so later, we were having a family dinner at my house and my mom came. As she entered the house, I was sitting in a chair in the family room and she looked at me thinking I was my brother. That freaked her out a little bit. It took my mom a few months to finally start getting use to my new look.

My appearance has changed. Even now several months later, I'm still getting used to my reflection. I like the way I look, but I'm not a fan of shaving. I don't like having to do that all the time. Here are a few fat bearded photos of me; one is a picture of me having an ice cream brain freeze with Mike in the background, the other is me at a park during a family picnic. Then there is a skinny bearded photo, and a skinny shaved face photo:

In the last three months there have been highs and lows. I left my job to seek a new career and different opportunities. As a person, I could see how I was feeling and responding differently to situations, good and bad, and how stress affected me. I noticed that worry wasn't a dominating feeling anymore. I have a knowledge that the Lord will always be there for me in every aspect of my life. I just have to put off the natural man and worldly concerns and remember that in the Lords time there *isn't time* for TV, overeating, or whatever it is that keeps me from doing what the Lord would have me do.

CHAPTER 13

The Marathon

THE CLIMAX, THE pinnacle, the race! I am actually going to run a marathon. In 10 months have I really gone from couch potato to running a marathon? What an amazing journey! It's hard for me to even believe.

A week or two before the race, the company putting on the event (Foot Traffic) had a pre-race run for those who had not previously registered. Those that participated in this run could enter their names for a drawing to get an entry in the sold out race. There were 10 spots that were going to be opened for the full marathon. This was the only way to get into the race at this time. By this point Ty had decided that he wanted to run the race with his wife Holly, his wife's sister, Annette Campbell, Scott, and I. I really wanted him to run it with us as well. It was actually very important to me. So he went to the run and after it was finished – he got selected for an entry! He paid the entry fee and secured his spot. I was thrilled he could run the race with Scott and me. It just felt right. Also miraculously David Neil and Greg Miller who go to church with Scott, Ty, and me were also able to secure marathon spots that evening. All three of them went that night, and the fact that they all got in was amazing. David was our Bishop and I was Greg's home teacher. What a blessing! There were many others that were at the run that evening and did not get in, but the 3 that I knew, did. Miracles do happen.

The week before the race I drove the course a couple of times. I wanted to familiarize myself with the turns and see how flat it really was. It is advertised as a very flat race. The first time I drove it Mel and the kids were with me having a little bit of family time. The second time Mel and I were on a motorcycle ride with her brother and his wife and we drove the course again as part of a longer ride we did that day. I was excited that the course was pretty flat and in a rural area on Sauvie's Island. It occurred to me that 26.2 miles is a LONG WAY! Even driving it took a long time, and I was going to run it.

4 or 5 days before the marathon I started carbo-loading. It was my first time trying to do this and I did it the complete wrong way. It was a disaster. I ate all the wrong things and was a little out of control. Right before I started carbo-loading, my daughter Jonaka was in Chicago for a choir festival with her school. She flew home with an authentic Chicago deep dish style pizza for me. She brought it in a special carry on cooler bag. I ate this as part of my carbo-loading. Here is a picture of it:

It was absolutely delicious. I approximate that about 300 of my previous 340 lbs was pizza, and it is by far my most favorite food. I used to eat pizza 3-4 days a week when I could. My record as a teenager was 12 meals straight of nothing but pizza – a full 4 days. I had never had real Chicago pizza and had always wanted it. So this was my chance and I took it. Besides I was carbo-loading, right? Over these days I also ate 5 donuts- basically all the wrong things.

The result of this caused me terrible gas pains, so bad that it even woke me up in the middle of the night. I thought my appendix had burst it hurt so bad. I took some gas relief pills and an hour or so later the pain subsided and I eventually fell back to sleep. This happened 2 nights in a row! I was definitely doing it all wrong. I was also constipated – feeling terrible. My system was backed up and nothing was coming out. I got so worried about the constipation that the day before the race I took a dose of milk of magnesia. Then I couldn't stop going to the bathroom and had the reverse problem. It lasted almost up to the start of the race. It was terrible. Needless to say, I learned exactly the way NOT to prepare for a race and how NOT to carbo-load. Lesson learned.

The day before the race I was a huge ball of energy. I remember going to see Scott at his office and just pacing the floor in front of one of his employees' desks unable to stop. I was jumping around and talking nonstop. I was so excited and juiced up. I wrote in my journal on the day before the race July 3rd, 2013:

"Tomorrow is the marathon and I'm buzzing nervous and am pacing and full of energy and adrenaline. So nervous."

I was bib number 2041. This is a picture of my bib. It is missing the tear off coupon for the free hot dog and strawberry shortcake.

The day of the race July 4th, 2013 I wrote in my journal:

"Independence Day and race day. Kind of fitting – my independence from obesity! I had a hard time sleeping last night, but

got a couple hours of sleep. I woke up about 2am and went to the bathroom then laid in bed for an hour and a half until I got up and showered and got ready. I'm now waiting for Ty to come pick Mike and me up. All morning long I have felt joy and happiness and the hymn "Master the Tempest is Raging" has been going through my head – "Peace, Peace be still…" I am so excited. I am texting everyone now and we are all ready. I am so excited."

I want to share all the details of the race so I will share my journal entry where I wrote all of the specifics of the race I could remember. I wrote this entry 2 days after the race on July 6th, 2013. I will insert pictures as appropriate.

"So I am up early at 4:30am and I want to write in my journal about the marathon. Mike came down and spent the night and slept on the couch. We talked a little but mostly just got to bed early. At 2am I was awake. Previous journal entry covers this. When Ty picked us up at 4:45am Holly, Annette and Richard, (Holly's sister and her husband) Scott, Greg, Bishop David Neil, Mike and I joined him in the van. We drove down to Portland for the race. We had no problem getting onto the island as we were early enough. We followed all the traffic and parked in a huge gravel lot, fairly close to the start/finish line.

There were huge lines all morning for the porta-potties. I got in one quickly and went #2 for the first time. I then went and picked up my event t-shirt and walked around for a bit, there were hundreds if not a couple thousand people there. The bib that I had picked up on Monday had all the info on the back, the race we were doing, the shirt size we ordered, name, age, and the electronic timing chip. I then went back to the car and put on a little sun screen and talked a little with the others — we took a picture.

(David Neil, Mike Riley, Greg Miller, Scott Gifford, Me, Ty & Holly Engstrom, & Annette Campbell)

I then had to pee, but at this point the bathroom lines were ridiculous with several hundred people waiting to use them. So I went into a big, old storage barn and peed in a corner. I'm glad I didn't get caught! I headed toward the starting line as they were starting to call for the runners. It was about 6:15am and the race for the full marathon started at 6:30. I found Scott and Ty and hugged them and told them I loved them. I went and found Mike as we were planning to start the race together. My goal for the race had been a 12 minute per mile pace so to finish in 5:15 hours with a stretch goal of 11:30 minute pace and finish under 5 hours. When I did my 23 mile run it was a 12 minute per mile pace.

The announcer got us fired up a little bit as we were all standing around the start area shoulder to shoulder. There were 439 racers or at least finishers and the race started at almost exactly 6:30am. I was very excited and nervous as I have written before. I had decided that I would do an interval of 2¾:1 minute for the race. It's the first time I had done that, but I wanted to do more than 2½:1 minute interval of my 23 mile run and the 3:1 minute interval I did on my 21 miler was my worst run, and I didn't want to recreate that run and let that psychological effect take over me.

So this huge herd of humans took off, it was exciting and so different running in a sea of people and bodies since running is really a solitary sport, it was very different. When we crossed the start line there is an electronic timing system and it beeped when you crossed it. I felt good physically at the beginning of the race. I started the chronograph on my watch; GPS phone program (Runtastic), and the interval timer on my watch. At the first 2:45 minute Mike and I did our first walk break and it felt funny as we pulled over to the right side of the road and a ton of people passed us, but I was determined to stick to the program. The first mile went great and we were on a great pace around 11:20 minute mile, so we didn't go out too fast and avoided that tendency that people have. Mile 2 was actually my fastest at 10 minutes, it felt great, but I knew I had to slow it down. And so it went, I would run for 2:45 minutes and walk for 1 minute.

Within the first few miles you kind of figure out whom you'll be running around and there were these 2 ladies Sandy and Joy that were super nice that I shared my weight loss story with, I was happy to do so. Sandy told me that this course is meticulously measured so staying on the inside of the corners will be the 26.22 miles. I found this to be true as my phone GPS actually calculated me running further than 26.2 miles and it always calculates less as it cuts corners when I run.

So mile 3 was great at 11:05 pace, 4 – great at 10:26 pace, 5 – still felt fantastic @ 10:45 pace, 6 – great at 11:02 pace, 7 – great at 10:37 pace, 8 – I felt great @ 10:38 pace. It was close to this point that I started to pull away from Mike a little bit. He was still behind me, but we weren't running together anymore. We had predetermined that we would run our own race, but would start out together.

(This is a picture I took with my phone while running)

These first 8 miles I constantly would pass and be passed by Bishop and we got to see each other. Also between mile 8 and 9 I had the inkling that I would have to go to the bathroom again (#2) and I wasn't happy. This was one of my biggest concerns as it was a huge contributor in my difficult 21 mile training run. So mile 9 I felt good at 10:43 pace and mile 10 still felt good, but I knew I would have to stop and poop. I wasn't happy, but at least there were toilets at the aid stations. Mile 10 was an 11:25 pace, my pace slowed down now some, as I had to go. Mile 10 was also the turnaround for the long out and back section of the course.

On another note I took a gel pack about every 45 minutes or so, taking 4 total over the race (I didn't take anymore after those 4). I drank water at every aid station and an electrolyte drink only twice. The first time I took it, it did not sit well in my stomach.

Mile 11 was good at 11:28 pace, there was a restroom (toilet) at an aid station close to there, but just before I got there another runner went in. I was very frustrated because I didn't want to wait for her, so I kept running. Mile 12 – 11:20 pace, it was an ok time, but I had to go. Then mile 13 was a 14:18 pace and was where I finally made it into the porta-potty. This is never a pleasant experience during a run. The long pace time includes the time I was on the toilet. While in the bathroom, I also noticed that some chafing had started to rub my privates raw and this really worried me. This had never happened before and I was only at the half way point of the race. My underwear had a bloody spot on them. So I finished my business and got going again, there was a poor lady that had to wait for me to get done with the toilet. Afterwards my bowels felt better and I was very glad for that. My privates were causing me concern as it was quite sore and continuing to rub, getting worse and there was nothing I could do.

It was also at this point around mile 13 that I stopped seeing Mike and Bishop.

(I was smiling for the camera at this point,

but felt worried)

Mile 14 was ok at 11:53 pace; mile 15 was ok at 11:09 pace. It was around this time that I started to feel my quads / thighs starting to hurt. I wasn't happy about this either as this is a little sooner than I wanted it to happen. So far I had to use the bathroom, raw privates, and my legs had started to hurt. Mile 16 was 11:46 pace and quads hurt but I was ok. Mile 17 was a 12:05 pace and I was feeling it. Mile 18 was an out and back up a little hill it was a 12:02 pace and I was hurting. Mile 19 was a 13:00 minute pace and a very difficult mile for me. I hit the point where I questioned for a second about finishing. I was in a lot of pain and still had 7-8 miles to go. I hit the proverbial wall. I shed some tears while running, drank some water at the aid station and poured some over my head and back. It was starting to heat up now as well making it harder, but I kept going.

Mile 20 was a little better at 11:44 pace, but I was in a lot of pain. Mile 21 at 13:12 minute pace — very difficult, but I was still sticking to my intervals at this point — my quads were killing me.

It was right at this point when I see my brother Lance and his wife Brandee on their bikes coming towards me. I needed that so bad. They rode alongside me for mile 22 at 11:25 pace, gave me an electrolyte capsule to take as I wasn't able to stomach the drink that was offered. I cried as I ran next to them and they encouraged me, it was great to have them there.

Also around mile 19 my stomach started hurting something awful, (lower left) causing me a lot of pain and difficulty running. I also knew that I had blisters on my left foot and toes. So now, painful quads, raw privates, stomach cramps, blisters, and the sun beating down on me. I needed that pick me up for a few minutes with Lance and Brandee. I didn't know that they were going to come, although I invited Lance personally he never committed to me that he would be there. Later Brandee told me that he had been planning all along to be there and he wanted to be, this makes me cry.

At mile 23, a 12:23 pace, I saw Mel and the kids on their bikes. It was funny because when they saw me they cheered and the lady in front of me raised her arms, taking encouragement from them. It was emotional to see them. I ran by them and Lance and Brandee took off and Mel and the kids finally came up along side me. At this point I was in so much pain my intervals had pretty much fallen apart and I was walking way more, probably closer to 2 minutes run and 2 minutes walk – it was sporadic and unscheduled.

One of the blisters popped on my foot which hurt worse now for some reason. While it was great to see my family it was also difficult for me to have them see me in so much pain and struggling. Not like when I was doing so good at the beginning of the race. I was moaning, groaning, and wincing in pain; a real struggle. Mile 24 was a 12:54 pace and mile 25 a 13:22 pace were my worst ones without having to stop for the bathroom break and Mel and Jonni

were with me those 2 miles. I felt terrible, everything was killing and even though I was close and I could see the barns at the finish, I felt like I couldn't make it.

I had asked Beyden to go check on Mike, which he did, and then at this point I asked the family to ride ahead and meet me at the finish line. I wanted them there when I finished and it was hard for me to have them see me in so much pain. I also passed Holly right around this point, walking with her and talking for a bit.

I remember thinking its time to run again and my mind is saying run and my body is saying NO!! Then in agony I started running again. Mile 26 at 12:49 pace I was by myself and my body was shot. As I came close to the finish and saw the van, I saw Ty and Scott and pointed at them and they took off toward the finish line. As I got closer, there were all my family and friends screaming and cheering for me. As I rounded the last corner to enter thru the arch amidst the outpouring of love I raised my arms and wept with joy, and for a second my pain was gone.

I finished 26.22 miles in an official time of 5 hours 6 minutes and 22 seconds when the electronic timing chip beeped. As I crossed the line I fell into Scott's arms and we embraced for many seconds weeping, I am so glad that he was the one that came to me first. He has been a pillar of strength to me spiritually and physically on this journey.

I then hugged Lance, Ty, then Mel, Jonaka, Beyden, and the rest of the family. Mom, Dad, Cari, Brian, Cohan, Emily, Brandee were all there. Also there were Marissa and Alisa, Scott and David's wives. Having all those there supporting me was wonderful at the end of the race, they doted on me. I could hardly walk and limped around. Holly came across a few minutes after me, then Bishop about 25 minutes after, and Mike about 45 minutes after me. We took pictures and all bonded.

Scott finished in 3 hours 28 minutes, Ty in 3 hours 55 minutes, Greg in 4 hours 22 minutes.

I had a final average pace of 11:41 minute miles and beat my goal of 5 hours 15 minutes. I was close to the 5 hour mark which would have been amazing. I took my shoes and socks off and got in a dirty kiddy pool with cold water for a few minutes and then put my socks back on and walked around in them for the rest of the day.

The lady at one of the tables recognized me from when I picked up my bib (I had shared my weight loss story with her) Mel went over and I showed her my before and after picture. She then told one of the people that run Foot Traffic about me and he came over and congratulated me and took me over to their booth and gave me a running shirt with 26.2 in big letters on it, saying he loved my story and congratulated me. I ate the strawberry shortcake and hot dog they had for us and basked in the joy and happiness at the finishers' line for a long time talking to family, friend, runners, volunteers, and workers at the race. I soaked it all in and was in no hurry to leave. I loved it! I shared my story with those it seemed fitting, too. I cheered Bishop and Mike as they crossed the finish line."

I wrote right after finishing the race in my journal as I had taken it to the event:

"I am in so much pain. Quads, toes (blisters), knees / joints, but I feel amazing. I almost constantly cried for an hour after I finished the race – Amazing to have everyone there."

"I DID IT!! I DID IT!! In just over 10 months I lost 135 lbs and went from zero activity to finishing a marathon!! I met my goal I set all those years ago, 6 years and then did nothing about until my 40th birthday, and in the process have changed physically and spiritually."

CHAPTER 14
Climbing the Mountain

WHAT BETTER WAY to celebrate running a marathon than by climbing Mt. St. Helens with Scott 4 days later! 3 days after the marathon I got a phone call from Scott inviting me to climb Mt. St. Helens the next morning. After a few gasps of air and visions of, "No way" going through my head, I couldn't form a good excuse not to, so I said yes. Again, I was nervous and excited. I spent that evening getting ready, trying to throw together all the things I would need for the climb. I had to borrow clothes and packs from my brother. Luckily I had a good pair of boots I had just bought for a backpacking trip I was doing with the scouts later in the summer. With some help I got everything together and tried to calm my nerves.

On July 16th, 2013, 8 days after the climb, I finally got around to writing it down in my journal.

"Let me start from the very beginning and write what I can remember. Scott picked me up at 7am, we were meeting one of his work clients (for his insurance business) in Woodland at 8am and he needed to stop by Winco and get his food for the day. I was pretty nervous at this point as I was thinking I would be the slow one in the party holding everyone up, as I have always been my entire life. When we got to Woodland and met up with Tom, he was 65 years old, a really nice guy, but I knew I was going to be ok.

We stopped in Cougar and signed in and got our climbing permit.

31033
Mount St. Helens National Volcanic Monument
Climbing Permit

Name TRENT HEPPLER

Issuing Officer LF

Date of Climb 7-8-13

Read and sign reverse side to validate permit.
Climbing fees are **not** refundable.

We got to the parking area at the base of the hikers path before 9am, we got all lathered up in sun screen and our packs ready and took off. In the first 10 minutes I knew that Tom was going to have trouble. The first couple of miles are fairly easy walking through the tree line. Tom was struggling and I was really surprised at myself that I wasn't more empathetic, as I have always been the one in Tom's situation and now that I wasn't I found that I was getting annoyed. This is definitively another personal characteristic for me to work on improving. We finally got through the trees and into climbing over some big rocks (very sharp) and it was a steeper ascent.

We were moving really slow with Tom struggling and it wasn't a workout at all for me. I was actually a little disappointed that I wasn't getting my heart rate up and my system energized. Scott and I hiked ahead of Tom and then stopped and waited for 15-20 minutes for Tom to catch up with us. I had decided there that I needed to tape my heels as it felt like they were getting blisters. So while we waited for Tom to recover after he caught us (he laid down), I got out my athletic tape and covered my heels good. After Tom got up he told us that he was going to drop his pack and just carry water in his pockets, and wanted us to go to the summit and he would meet us there. If we didn't see him after 1-1½ hours to come back and find him. We had been hiking for approximately 2½ hours at this point and gone maybe halfway. We hadn't gotten to the snow or the real loose rock that you slide back on when you walk up it.

At this point Scott and I took off and it felt great to get the heart rate up. I was pretty much keeping up with him, he would pull ahead of me but the couple times he stopped he only had to wait for a few minutes. Fairly soon after we departed we came to the snow and I followed Scott straight up the mountain as we made our own path in the snow. This allowed us to pass all the difficult loose gravel everyone else was hiking through.

We must have passed 25-35 people during this time. I was amazed at how well I was doing. I mean there were all these people climbing this mountain that were fit enough to do it and I was there passing them. It was very empowering. After a while Scott had stopped for me and when I caught him he told me that we had just climbed 2000 steps in that last push. It was awesome. So off we went and after 1½ hours I made it to the summit. I really got in a rhythm with my steps, breathing, trekking poles, and just kept pushing. My body was carrying me up this mountain."

This is the link and QR code of the video I took when I made the summit: http://bit.ly/powerwithin5

"So we did the second half of the mountain in a great time. Scott had probably been waiting for 5 minutes or so at the top. At the summit we took pictures, talked and it was awesome being at the rim of this mountain with the crater below us and the volcano steaming out of the dome. We even laid down and took a nap at the summit – IT WAS AMAZING!

I had packed up some sweat pants, spandex leggings, and a coat. I put them all on at the top as it was windy and cold and the sweat I had generated was chilling me. I was very glad and fortunate to have all of the equipment I had and borrowed. It was perfect.

After an hour and a half there was no sign of Tom so we got out the black plastic garbage bags, ripped leg holes in them, and put them on like a diaper. We then put our packs on our fronts and glissaded down the mountain on our butts. It was incredible and so fun. You could control your speed by laying back to go faster or sitting up to slow down. My garbage bag eventually ripped and I was sliding on my sweat pants, but I didn't care. Eventually we had to stop and traverse over quite a ways back to the marked path. Scott picked the perfect line and we ended up exactly where Tom was. There I took *off all my long pants and coat and packed them up and we headed down. The hike down was very pleasant with a great conversation with Scott about my hunting/guiding adventures in Saskatchewan.*

We had to wait from time to time for Tom to catch up to us, but it was so beautiful, I was grateful we could take our time going down. At the tree line we found a great spot to sit in the shade and talk.

A number of times I said to Scott, "It's about the journey."
How accurate. I took many pictures. I love them. It was amazing —

a great experience and I loved celebrating my marathon by climbing a mountain."

After the climb I had posted a status on Facebook about it with a few pictures and stated what a wonderful way it was to celebrate completing a marathon. I got a few comments, but my favorite was from my brother, who commented, "We can ride to the coast tomorrow, then swim to Japan." I thought this was hilarious – loved it. I thought that was a great idea.

A week or so later I left with the Varsity Scout Team on a high adventure 4 day backpacking trip, hiking about 30 miles. I carried my journal and book outline with me on the backpacking trip, never writing in them, but they did make the journey with me. A while after getting back I finally wrote about the trip in my journal in the July 31st, 2013 entry. I will share parts of it.

"We left Monday morning at 5am from the church, those that went were leaders Dana Jensen, Drew Hansen, and I. Boys were Beyden, Kyler, Jacob N., Jake S., Cameron, and Carter. Everyone had received their food and other items at the Wednesday pack check – we were prepared. We got to Eagle Creek Trail Head at about 6:30am and loaded up and headed out. It was a beautiful hike. Day

one we passed Punchbowl Falls and Tunnel Falls where we walked thru a tunnel behind the falls — very cool. We ate lunch a little further down the trail at Twister Falls. There was a little pool at Twister Falls and a number of us swam in it. It was awesome.

A little further down the trail we camped at 7½ mile camp where we found a good spot close to the creek. We swam and played in the water where the highlight was getting under a powerful 6-9 foot waterfall with just enough room for 1 and experiencing the power of that water coming over you. The boys that were there all did it. It was really cool. I loved being there with Beyden.

That night at campfire/fireside Beyden led an excellent meeting.

I had asked him to give a spiritual thought and then he really did the rest. He had someone select a hymn and prayer and this set the tone for the other campfires/firesides each night. The boys had complained a lot during the day because it was hard and it hurt carrying the heavy packs. All of the firesides focused on how through doing hard things we learn the most and there is opposition in all things. We need to know the bad to know the good. Beyden did a great job and is amazing; I love him and Jonaka so much.

Day two we packed up and kept heading uphill on the trail to Wahtum Lake. This day was a lot of elevation gain, we hiked essentially 1 mile vertical over the 2 days, and the boys complained — A LOT! I finally had enough, and at one of the stopping points I told them they were acting like little kids and I wasn't their mother and didn't want to hear the murmuring and complaining any more and they needed to grow up. It was something they needed to hear. The adult leaders were hurting too, but showed a great example not complaining. The boys were quiet for the next hour or so after this.

We finally made it to the lake and found a campsite. After a few hours the boys were having a great time looking for crawdads and picking huckleberries. It was great that we were able to have fun at camps after the hard hikes. We had another wonderful fireside and a lot of testimonies were born by many. That night we started to come together as a quorum and leaders and had a fun conversation. I was very happy about this.

Day 3 we left and hiked to the base of Chinidere Mountain dropped our packs and climbed the summit. I ran and power walked up it. (That felt great). The view up there was spectacular. We saw all of the mountains in the area and eventually they all made it to the top. We took photos and enjoyed ourselves.

(Me and Beyden with Mt. Hood in the background)

This day on the trail we had great conversation going and very little complaining. It was nice and all recognized the joy and fellowship through the pain. We made it to our next campsite, camp Smokey which was a burned out part of the forest and very beautiful in a different way. Water was scarce here, but I was glad we had a trickle of a stream. That evening's fireside was amazing with much testimony shared. Beyden even cried. It was the first time I can remember hearing him cry with emotion from the spirit. Many bore testimony and it was wonderful. The rest of the evening was filled with great group conversation.

(I guess I like to hike in white tech shirts
and black shorts! – Whatever works right?)

*Day 4 we got going and hiked through more beautiful forest with
great views. We hiked on and down some really steep hills the rest of
the day – it was very difficult. About a 4000 ft. drop in 1 mile. It
was super steep and kind of scary. Many slipped, but there were no
injuries and we all made it. We came back to the cars in high spirits
and headed home."*

It was a difficult but great experience that I have
reflected on many times with the boys.

The next week I drove to Camp Meriwether to spend 3 days with the Boy Scout Troop. It was great to be there and serve these younger boys. A couple of them that were there also went on the backpacking trip. At the last minute I was needed as a leader and I was glad that I went. Honestly, I wasn't too excited when I first got asked, as I had just spent 4 difficult, if not grueling, days with a bunch of young boys, but I really enjoyed it when I got there. I have been to scout camp many times as a leader, but this time was different. While there I participated in a lot of the fun activities like the polar bear swim, (which is actually in the ocean) the scoutmaster shootout, (both rifle and bow), and a couple of the tours offered in the evenings. These are things I never did in the past, before my transformation, probably because it was more physically and emotionally demanding and I would have been tired. I was so glad I did this time.

I shared my story a few times while at camp with those that I felt I should. One of the people I shared it with was Mark Dorrough who is a fellow marathoner. I really cherished my conversation with him. I really love it when the Spirit touches me to share my story with others and it feels like the right thing for me to do.

When I go camping (that is if I'm not on a

backpacking trip) I have a cot and sleeping bag system that is second to none. When I was fat, the only way I could get any sleep was to have an amazing set up. Beyden calls me a high maintenance camper, and he is right. This is a picture of my scout camp pack, 90% of which is my sleeping gear. This includes; cot, sleeping bag, pillows, blanket, & foam mats. My sleeping bag is so large and awesome that it takes 3 guys to get it back in its compression sack. It is the item on the very top of the pack. That was one heavy pack!

What a blessing it was to be able to physically accomplish these rewards, experiences, and service opportunities. What a blessing it was to be unemployed that I had the time to be able to do so. What a blessing it is to be spiritually edified and to, hopefully, edify others through these experiences.

CHAPTER 15
The Final Weigh-in

365 DAYS – THE one year mark. Truly what a difference a year can make. It was my birthday and I was turning 41 years old. My fourth and final weigh-in was about to happen. At 3am that morning (August 23rd, 2013) I got a text from Scott asking me to meet him at a local breakfast restaurant to celebrate. I thought this was weird that 1) he would text me in the middle of the night, and 2) that I would hear the vibration and notification sound from my cell phone out of my deep sleep and read the text. But I did answer. I texted him back agreeing to his suggestion, I thought it sounded wonderful. He texted back and said "Great! See you then! Happy Birthday! Mission Accomplished!" That was a fantastic text to receive. Later

Scott told me that he too woke out of a deep sleep to send me that message.

That morning I weighed myself before I met Scott for breakfast at 7:45am. I weighed-in at 194.2 lbs. My goal was 195 lbs. I had lost 138.2 lbs! For the last month I had ranged between 193-198 lbs, so I was glad that on that day I had met my goal again. I was really happy. I met Scott for breakfast and I ate delicious eggs benedict and 1 pancake. It was great. At the restaurant Scott filmed the final video on his cell phone. Here is the link and QR code: http://bit.ly/powerwithin6

That day I got many birthday wishes by phone, in person, and on social media. But the one that really turned on the faucet of tears was from my daughter Jonaka. She wrote to me: "Dad it's your birthday, and what a different one it is! This day last year you decided to change your body, but today we see a fully changed man. Not only did you lose weight, but you gained so much. You gained a soft heart, a willing mind, a fun attitude, and an aware spirit. You are an inspiration to so many people! So today is your special day, but remember, you're special everyday. I love you, happy birthday!"

This was the day when it really sunk in that I had met my goals; even exceeded some of them and reached others I didn't know I had set. I just knew I needed to change. The journey never was an easy one – it was a joyous one.

President Thomas S. Monson in the November 2008 Ensign article "Finding Joy in the Journey" says, "Let us relish life as we live it, find joy in the journey, and share our love with friends and family. One day each of us will run out of tomorrows… This is our one and only chance at mortal life – here and now. The longer we live, the greater is our realization that it is brief. Opportunities come, and then they are gone. I believe that among the greatest lessons we are to learn in this short sojourn upon the earth are lessons that help us distinguish between what is important and what is not. I plead with you not to let those most important things pass you by as you plan for that illusive and nonexistent future when you will have time to do all that you want to do. Instead, find joy in the journey – now." How true these words sing. I started this journey with a goal to run a marathon and in the process have done things with my life that have improved it multiple times over.

For my 41st birthday present I got a road bike from Mel and my family. When I got back from the backpacking trip with the Varsity Scouts, there it was in the living room. It was a road bike I had looked at before I had left. It was used, but new to me! I was so excited. My sisters, brother, and parents were invited by Mel to help buy the present and I love it. I have really enjoyed riding for the first time in my life.

I knew how to ride a bike from when I was a child, but this was a whole different story. The very first time I "clipped in" I was so nervous. I had borrowed shoes from Ty and was sitting on the bike in my garage with my left foot clipped in, holding onto a freezer with my left hand. Paralyzed with fear, I must have sat there for at least 2 minutes before I finally pushed off. I started going and clipped in my right foot.

I found that wearing a pair of bike shorts wasn't enough padding for me, so I went out in the garage and found some car wax applicator pads, the round ones about the size of your palm and stuck a couple of those in the bike shorts for some extra padding. They worked great and I could just throw them in the washing machine when dirty.

One of the longer rides I have been on was the same bridges loop I did on my 23 mile run. However, I started at my own house and not my brother's, so the ride was more than 31 miles. On this ride I was coming up to a cross walk and asked the guy standing there to hit the button to activate the signal. As he did, I took my right foot out of the clip to stop and then proceeded to fall to the left. I couldn't get my foot out in time so I heeded the advice that my riding friends had told me, which was to not put my arm out and avoid breaking my wrist and just fall on my side. It hurt for sure but was mostly embarrassing. The guy there freaked out a little and the cars at the intersection got a good show. I couldn't get out of there fast enough when the signal finally turned, I was so embarrassed. Even though I went through that experience, I still enjoy the bike.

For Labor Day 2013 we went camping with my family as we usually do up at Swift Reservoir near Mt. St. Helens. My sister always brings their ski boat. All of my life, from when I was a kid, my dad had tried to get me to water ski, but I could never get up. This went on for years until he finally gave up. My sister has tried multiple times to get me up water skiing as an adult, but these attempts have been unsuccessful as well. She even sat me on the inner-tube and towed me along, trying to get me up that way, but to no avail. But, in her true form she asked me again, and even though I didn't want to, I agreed to give it another shot. I wasn't concerned if I got up because I had long ago decided that my life would be plenty fulfilled without ever water skiing. But what do you know? I got right up - and on the very first try. I had a permagrin on my face the whole time and I was loving it. I went for a good long time and even crossed the wake. Here is a video with terrible quality, but cool audio (you can hear me whooping in the background): http://bit.ly/powerwithin7

And here is a picture:

The whole family – Mel, Jonaka, Beyden, and I had a great time on the water that day with my sister and brother-in-law.

From the very beginning – day 1 of my journey and periodically throughout, I have taken my measurements. I have measured my right arm around the bicep, my shoulders, chest, stomach (what use to be known as the black hole), and my right thigh. I want to share them, so you can see the progression over the year.

Date:	8-28-12	10-6-12	11-23-12	1-20-13	2-24-13	5-19-13	8-27-13	Loss
R. Arm:	18"	18.5"	16"	16"	15.5"	13"	12.5"	5.5"
Shoulder:	55"	56.5"	52.5"	51.25"	48.5"	47"	46.5"	10"
Chest:	56"	54.25"	50.75"	47.5"	45.25"	42"	41"	15"
Stomach:	58"	56"	53.25"	49"	46.5"	42.5"	41"	17"
R. Thigh:	27.25"	26.5"	22.25"	25"	23"	22"	21.75"	5.5"

That's a total loss of 53.5" with just these 5 measurements. I now fit comfortably into a 34-35 pant and a medium or large shirt. That is just unbelievable to me.

In this process I have been unemployed or underemployed through most of it. In June 2013 I parted ways with my job as a Dental Manager and was again unemployed. I was told through inspired witnesses that I would get a new career. In my July 31st, 2013 journal entry

I wrote:

"I do want to write that 3 priesthood holders have born witness to me that I will be blessed and find a job. First was president Hess (Elders Quorum) was over on Thursday and he was impressed to tell me as he was leaving that the Lord will bless me and my family, and I will find a job. He added it may not be what I expect or something to that effect. Also Scott and Gordon both felt impressed by the spirit to tell me that I would be blessed with a job/work by my willingness to come to scout camp."

On September 12th, 2013 I started a new career. I am very excited and am seeing the Lord's blessings.

What a spectacular year! Yet still at times when I picture myself in my head I see the fat guy, and am often surprised by my reflection. I feel a kinder, more loving, less worried, more service-oriented (Christlike) person coming to life. My spiritual vision is clearer and my heart is more willing.

Here are a couple after pictures:

(ME AND MY JOURNAL)

CHAPTER 16
Relapse

I WISH I could say that this journey has been wonderful and fantastic without any difficult times, but that isn't life or my journey. I know that relapse has a place in overcoming addiction. Please understand that I do not use that as an excuse to have a relapse or fall back into addiction. I want to share an example of what a relapse looks like and how it affected me.

It starts with a very small step for me which is a thought – giving myself permission to indulge just a little bit more than I should. My first relapse's progression started on the backpacking trip with the Varsity Scouts. I had bought the same food for everyone to eat and carry in their packs. This included me. I remember being excited that I would have 4 days of eating all these foods like protein bars, jerky, trail mix, and bagels, without having to eat less than the others. I had counted on 4000-5000 calories a day for each hiker to make up for the loss of energy. I didn't gain any weight on this trip; I actually probably lost a little bit because of all the physical activity. I had also logged all of the food on MFP before I left so everything was accounted for with my intake. But after the trip I didn't like having to "go back" to the portion control and making better choices.

I was also at my goal weight between 193-198 lbs and struggling with this nonexistent mind set called "maintenance mode." The reality is that this is a complete change and I will never have a maintenance mode. I'm just always adjusting to what my body needs – it never ends. I think many get caught in the trap of thinking there is a resting place called maintenance mode, where you don't have to focus and keep working. This does not exist. I believe in the saying that if you are not moving forward than you are moving backwards. You can never just stay still.

This reminds me of my favorite book by Dr. Seuss "Oh, the Places You'll Go" where he describes the waiting place:

"headed, I fear, toward a most useless place.

The Waiting Place…

…for people just waiting.

Waiting for a train to go

or a bus to come, or a plane to go

or the mail to come, or the rain to go

or the phone to ring, or the snow to snow

or waiting around for a Yes or No

or waiting for their hair to grow.

Everyone is just waiting.

Waiting for the fish to bite

or waiting for wind to fly a kite

or waiting around for Friday night

or waiting, perhaps, for their Uncle Jake

or a pot to boil, or a Better Break

or a string of pearls, or a pair of pants

or a wig with curls, or Another Chance.

Everyone is just waiting.

NO!

That's not for you!

Somehow you'll escape

all that waiting and staying."

My relapse continued and sometime after getting back from scout camp I started thinking about sneaking food. For me, when I hide something, that's when my addiction is back and I'm in a relapse. I hadn't actually hidden anything or snuck any food yet, but I was thinking about it.

Those thoughts worked on me for a few weeks until one day I was out getting bread for groceries, and there was this free piece of carrot cake – a big piece. I got it, thinking I would give it to Beyden. Deep down I knew he wouldn't eat it.

I had eaten the whole thing in my truck before I made it home. I ate it without any utensil, just shoving it in my mouth with my hands. As disturbing as that is to write, I still didn't realize I was in relapse. I justified it as I could eat that now. I work out now; I am at my goal weight, and etc, etc, etc… I didn't tell anybody about the carrot cake, but thought to myself afterwards that I shouldn't have done that and wouldn't do it again. Relapses are not fun.

Well, my food addiction relapse wasn't over. A bit later I went to Little Caesars to get pizza for Beyden, Mel, and I for dinner. It was after 8pm and we wanted the deep dish pizza, so it wasn't "hot-n-ready" and took about 8 minutes. While there, I got an order of crazy bread. I ate the entire order of crazy bread and sauce – shoving it in as fast as I could. I wanted to eat all the evidence. It was a pretty dark moment, sitting in the car, just dipping and chewing. This is when I finally realized that I had been in relapse and needed to break the cycle. It was a low point.

I have learned that for me, breaking the cycle means to confess and forsake what I have done. To get out from behind the dark cloud and tell my secrets. The next day I told Mel and posted it on a MyFitnessPal status, and broke the cycle. I have to be so vigilant in not letting the thoughts start because that's where it all begins. When I have these thoughts I have to confess them to Mel and stop them in their tracks. I think this same pattern is similar with many addictions.

This brings me to another point. For many months now – almost like clockwork and almost everyday, what I call the "old Trent" comes out. He is short tempered, unkind, angry, selfish, and all the other characteristics that could be described as my worst behaviors. I very regretfully had saved my worst behaviors for those I love the most. For this I am very sorry. I think most people that I interact with outside of my immediate family saw my better characteristics and they might be surprised by that. It's hard to face these things and share my dark personal traits. I do so now because by sharing, I believe it will help me to improve, be better, and also give hope to others with the same problem.

Sometimes I don't know why he – "the old Trent" – even comes out. The oddest, littlest things trigger him, and he roars out as I struggle to put him away. However, the more I put him away and the faster I do it, the less he shows his ugly head. I have to apologize to my loved ones and let them know that I need to continue to focus on the kinder, gentler Trent. The Trent the Lord wants me to be – meek. Sharing this story hasn't always been pretty, but it has always been real. I hope that my journey and experiences can help someone get through their own journey.

CHAPTER 17

The Power Within

CHRIST IS THE power within, and only through him can you or I change. Moroni chapter 7 verse 12 in The Book of Mormon says, "All things which are good cometh from God." I know this to be true.

One of the blessings I have had the last few months is sharing my story with those that ask and when I feel prompted. This has helped me to remember the process and reminds me to continue moving forward. Just like I mentioned before, we are always either moving forward or backward, there is no "waiting place." This includes physically, emotionally, and spiritually. With the physical body, there are rest days in training which are necessary to help the body heal and grow stronger. I equate these to times of reflection and review on an emotional and spiritual level – the key to growth though, is you must act on what's being taught and what you are learning. As I've shared my story it has recommitted me to the process and doing the Lords will. I see this as being valiant in my testimony of Jesus Christ.

Bruce R. McConkie in the November 1974 Ensign Pg. 35 shared what it means to be valiant in a testimony of Jesus Christ.

"What does it mean to be valiant in the testimony of Jesus? It is to be courageous and bold; to use all our strength, energy, and ability in the warfare with the world; to fight the good fight of faith. ... The great cornerstone of valiance in the cause of righteousness is obedience to the whole law of the whole gospel. To be valiant in the testimony of Jesus is to 'come unto Christ, and be perfected in him'; it is to deny ourselves 'of all ungodliness,' and 'love God' with all our 'might, mind and strength.' (Moroni 10:32)

To be valiant in the testimony of Jesus is to believe in Christ and his gospel with unshakable conviction. It is to know of the verity and divinity of the Lord's work on earth. But this is not all. It is more than believing and knowing. We must be doers of the word and not hearers only. It is more than lip service; it is not simply confessing with the mouth the divine Sonship of the Savior. It is obedience and conformity and personal righteousness...

To be valiant in the testimony of Jesus is to 'press forward with a steadfastness in Christ, having a perfect brightness of hope, and a love of God and of all men.' It is to 'endure to the end.' (2 Nephi 31:20) It is to live our religion, to practice what we preach, to keep the commandments. It is the manifestation of 'pure religion' in the lives of men; it is visiting 'the fatherless and widows in their affliction' and keeping ourselves 'unspotted from the world.' (James 1:27.)

To be valiant in the testimony of Jesus is to bridle our passions, control our appetites, and rise above carnal and evil things. It is to overcome the world as did He who is our prototype and who Himself was the most valiant of all our Father's children. It is to be morally clean, to pay our tithes and offerings, to honor the Sabbath day, to pray with full purpose of heart, to lay our all upon the altar if called upon to do so.

To be valiant in the testimony of Jesus is to take the Lord's side on every issue. It is to vote as he would vote. It is to think what he thinks, to believe what he believes, to say what he would say and do what he would do in the same situation. It is to have the mind of Christ and be one with him as he is one with his Father."

How powerful is that?! How clear, how simple - how hard – right? This is the journey we take in life. I can tell you one thing for sure – "it is easier to run with the Lord, than without him!" Mike Riley told me that years ago. This is true in reality and figuratively. The times I spent on my long runs and the spirit that was with me are precious, sacred, and full of learning experiences. Those were times when I was exhausted and in pain, but the spirit lifted my body, making me move forward. It is a wonderful truth.

During the same camping trip where I water skied for the first time, I was talking with my sister and parents. It occurred to me why this was happening in my life *now*. It is because of the hastening of the work. In Doctrine and Covenants section 88 verse 73 it reads: "Behold, I will hasten my work in its time." I believe now is that time, not just because the age for missionaries has lowered and more are accepting calls to go on full time missions, but because the Lords needs ME to share His truths in whatever way I can. My journey has made His truths so much more real and rich in my life than they ever have been. I hope and pray that I may share with just 1 person, something that will help them to love the Lord more.

President Lorenzo Snow said in the Teachings of Presidents of the Church: Lorenzo Snow in chapter 11 "I Seek Not Mine Own Will, but the Will of the Father" – "We came into the world for a great purpose, the same as Jesus, our elder brother, to do the will and works of our Father; in this there is peace, joy and happiness, an increase of wisdom, knowledge and the power of God; outside of this are no promised blessings. Thus let us devote ourselves to righteousness, help each and all to be better and happier; do good to all and evil to none; honor God and obey His Priesthood; cultivate and preserve an enlightened conscience and follow the Holy Spirit; faint not, hold fast to what is good, endure to the end, and your cup of joy shall be full even to overflowing, for great shall be your reward for your trials and your sufferings and temptations, your fiery ordeals, your heart yearnings and tears; yea, our God will give you a crown of unfading glory." – Amen.

CONCLUSION

A YEAR IN the life of a middle aged man – one that has transformed me in so many ways. My daughter said it best in her birthday wish to me and I quote again, "Dad it's your birthday, and what a different one it is! This day last year you decided to change your body, but today we see a fully changed man. Not only did you lose weight, but you gained so much. You gained a soft heart, a willing mind, a fun attitude, and an aware spirit. You are an inspiration to so many people! So today is your special day, but remember you're special everyday. I love you." I love my daughter so much and am so thankful for her, my wife, and my son. I hope that I will be the father and husband they deserve.

As you contemplate, start, or continue your own journey, always remember that God loves you. You are His child. He has given you a Savior that you may return to live with Him. I bear my witness to you that I know He is real. He lives and loves you and me. The power within comes from Jesus Christ and through Him your life may be transformed.

RESOURCES

Book of Mormon – www.lds.org

Doctrine and Covenants of the Church of Jesus Christ of Latter-Day Saints – www.lds.org

Ensign of the Church of Jesus Christ of Latter-Day Saints – November 1974, Bruce R. McConkie "Be Valiant in the Fight of Faith" – www.lds.org

Ensign of the Church of Jesus Christ of Latter-Day Saints – November 2008, Thomas S. Monson "Finding Joy in the Journey" – www.lds.org

Free Dictionary – www.freeDictionary.com

Grandpa Bill's General Authority Pages – Neal A. (Ash) Maxwell 1926-2004 – www.gapages.com/maxwena1.htm

"He Did Deliver Me from Bondage" by Colleen C. Harrison – Windhaven Publishing & Productions ©2002

Jeff Galloway Website – www.jeffgalloway.com

"Mormon Doctrine" by Bruce R. McConkie

MyFitnessPal – www.myfitnesspal.com

"Oh, the Places You'll Go!" by Dr. Seuss – Random House New York ©1990

Runner's World "Running On Air: Breathing Technique" by Budd Coates and Claire Kowalchik, March 6th, 2013 – www.runnersworld.com

Teachings of Presidents of the Church: Lorenzo Snow. "I Seek Not Mine Own Will, but the Will of the Father" – www.lds.org

Made in the USA
San Bernardino, CA
02 February 2018